The Miracle Question

Answer It and Change Your Life

Linda Metcalf, PhD

Crown House Publishing Limited

www.crownhouse.co.uk

First published by

Crown House Publishing Ltd
Crown Buildings, Bancyfelin, Carmarthen, Wales, SA33 5ND, UK
www.crownhouse.co.uk

and

Crown House Publishing Company, LLC
4 Berkeley Street, 1st Floor, Norwalk, CT 06850, USA
www.CHPUS.com

British Library Cataloguing-in-Publication Data
A catalogue entry for this book is available
from the British Library.

ISBN 1904424260

LCCN 2004106210

To my husband Roger, and children, Kelli, Ryan and Roger Jr.

You are my miracle.

Contents

Acknowledgments

Someone once said that Walt Disney's huge empire began with a little mouse. Having been enchanted with his creativity since I was a child, I once read about his struggles and determination to pursue his dream and quickly learned that he had many problems to overcome. One could almost say that his "miracle" was to create entertainment so that people could escape from life and experience fantasy, just for a short while. His cartoons, movies, books and amusement parks brought people together from around the world, and together, they played.

I have thought about writing this book for a long time. I wanted to write it in a simple way that could give people a chance to escape from their problems, if only for a moment, so that they too, could dream and play. I wanted to give them hope and a belief that they were competent and could get past the problems in their way. To accomplish that, I needed support from a publisher, therapists who inspired me and clients who answered The Miracle Question and convinced me that it was a project worth pursuing.

Many thanks go to Mark Tracten, Director of US Operations for Crown House Publishing for believing in this work and steering me towards the people who could make it happen. Thanks to David Bowman, Managing Director, Rosalie Williams, Caroline Lenton and Clare Jenkins, for your help. Your kindness, prompt attention and patience with me have been greatly appreciated.

Thanks to the clients who allowed me to step into their lives, ask The Miracle Question and give me answers that were both surprising and exciting. It is you who have made this book possible. Your influence is on every page and your success continues to invigorate me daily as a therapist and instructor. Thank you to Mark Tally for his kindness in listening to me talk about this book and relating his experiences with the question.

Thanks to Steve deShazer, for first coining The Miracle Question, and Eve Lipchik, Insoo Berg, Michelle Weiner-Davis and Scott Miller for their continuous work in developing solution focused therapy. Thank you to Michael White and David Epston, two therapists whose work with Narrative Therapy blends so well with solution focused therapy that I can hardly imagine doing therapy without your influence. To Bill O'Hanlon, who has always supported my pursuits, thank you for the lovely foreword. When I was writing my first book ten years ago, it was you who said to me, "there are many ideas out there and lots of room at the top … go for it!" You practice what you preach.

Thanks finally, to my family, who are always supportive and understanding when deadlines come and I need to shut the door. To our oldest son, Roger Jr., thanks for telling me to go back and write the first chapter over and over until it sounded as if I was simply talking to the reader. I guess your Baylor degree paid off! Thanks to my daughter, Kelli for always making sure I took shopping therapy breaks. To my youngest son, Ryan, who kept me laughing and distracted with your drumming. And to my husband, Roger, thanks for always reminding me to save my manuscript late at night. To my parents, thanks for teaching me to never give up and to my brother, Bob thanks for reading the manuscript and giving me a thumbs up. Finally, thanks to my dog, Rex, who sat and waited patiently for his walk each night until the next page was finished. I am lucky to walk in this miracle with all of you.

Foreword

In 1990, I attended a large psychotherapy conference in Anaheim, California. The keynote address was given by Dr. Victor Frankl, a therapist I had long admired. Frankl told a story during this talk that mesmerized me. He had been imprisoned by the Nazi's during World War II. He had been transferred to four different concentration camps, watched his father die in one of the camps and been separated from his mother and his wife. His life as a psychiatrist, writer and lecturer had been interrupted by his imprisonment. He held the view that spirituality and meaning were central to mental health, an idea that was new at the time. Before he had a chance to write about this new idea, he was arrested and imprisoned. He was determined to survive the war if at all possible not only to find his surviving family, but to propagate this idea.

On a wintry day in Poland, while interred in his fourth concentration camp, Frankl was being marched through a field with a group of other prisoners. He was dressed in thin clothing, with no socks, and he had holes in his shoes. Very ill from malnutrition and mistreatment, he began to cough. The cough was so severe that he fell to his knees. A guard came over and told him to get up and keep walking, but he could not even answer as his cough was so intense and debilitating. The guard began to beat him with a club and told him that he would be left to die if he did not get up. Dr. Frankl knew the guard was deadly serious as he had witnessed the same done to other prisoners. Sick, in pain, and being hit, he thought, "This is it for me." He didn't have the wherewithal to get up.

There he was on the ground in no condition to go on, and all of a sudden he was no longer in Poland. Instead, he found himself imagining himself standing at a lectern in post-war Vienna giving a lecture on "The Psychology of Death Camps and the Psychology of Meaning". He held an audience of 200 rapt with attention. The lecture was one that he had been working on the whole time he had been in the prison camps. He spoke about how some people, those who find meaning and a connection to a higher purpose, seem to survive the experience psychologically and emotionally better than others. It was a brilliant lecture, all taking place in his mind's eye and ear. He was no longer half-dead in the field but living in the lecture. During the lecture, he told the imaginary audience about the day Victor Frankl was in that field being beaten and was certain he didn't have the strength to get up and keep walking.

Then, wonder of wonders, he told his imagined audience, he was able to stand up. The guard stopped beating him and he began, haltingly at first, then with more strength, to walk. As he was imagining describing this to his audience, his body got up and began to walk. He continued to imagine this lecture all the while he was doing the work detail and through the cold march back to the death camp. He collapsed into his bunk, imagining this brilliantly clear speech ending and him getting a standing ovation. Many years later and thousands of miles away, in 1990 in Anaheim, California, he received a standing ovation from 7,000 people after this speech.

What did Viktor Frankl do that most people with problems don't do? He vividly imagined a future in which his problems were resolved and then worked backwards to the present to determine what he would need to do in order to make that future a reality. I knew this "future strategy" well from my own life.

When I was in college, I became very depressed. I thought of myself as a poet and was so sensitive that I found it painful to be around people. At the same time, I was very lonely, and wanted very much to be with people. But when I was around people, I was so shy that I wouldn't say the things I wanted to say, or when I would talk, I was so nervous that I would say something I didn't mean to say.

I began to despair about my future, knowing that someday, college would be over and I would have to get a job, because my poetry probably wouldn't support me (for one thing, I was too frightened of rejection to show it to anyone, which made it very hard to get published, to say the least!). I couldn't see myself having a real job or working for some soul-numbing corporation.

After months of being depressed, I decided after much consideration, to kill myself. I had only a few friends and they were generally as miserable and estranged as I was, but I decided the only civil thing to do was to tell them of my plans and to say goodbye. The first two friends I told were sympathetic and told me that they felt the same way but didn't have the courage to take their own lives; they told me they admired my courage. My third, and last, friend, however, became very upset when I told her of my suicidal plans (she was a bit better adjusted). When I explained my reasons for taking my life, she made me an offer. She had some unmarried, childless aunts who lived in the Midwest who had told her she would inherit their estates when they died, as she was their favorite niece. Each of them had invested in local farmland and each farm had an empty farmhouse that was available. If I promised not to kill myself, my friend said, she would let me live rent-free in one of these houses for the rest of my life. I could write poetry, be away from the world and people, and grow my own food if I wanted, so I wouldn't have to work to earn a living (in my uninformed state at that time I thought I could actually pull this unlikely scheme off).

The plan seemed plausible and I noticed I was instantly no longer suicidal, because relief was promised for the future. I agreed to stay alive until one of the aunts died (they were in their sixties, and at 19, I was certain one of them was going to go soon). However, I still had a problem—I was miserable and didn't know how to get along in the world very well. It was then that I became obsessed with discovering how people lived successfully, that is, how they weren't miserable all the time like I was, how they got along with other people, and how they handled money, which was a chronic problem for me.

While it took me years to climb out of that depression, my obsession with how people become less miserable led me to investigate psychotherapy. Eventually, I became so interested in psychotherapy that I majored in psychology in my undergraduate university studies and went on to get an advanced degree in therapy.

I became a very passionate therapist, tracking down every approach with strict criteria: I was interested in therapeutic approaches that were practical and could help people actually change, rather than merely giving them or their therapists an explanation for their problems. This passion for effectiveness (and later for respectfulness when I discovered the covert distrust and disdain that some therapists and theories had for clients and patients) turned towards educating my fellow therapists. I began to travel around the world teaching seminars and went on from there to write many books in the field of therapy.

I never did go to live on one of those Aunt's farms in the Midwest, but having that future to live for led me to other futures. In this book, Linda Metcalf provides you with tools to change your life and relationships for the better using a simple and powerful future method, The Miracle Question. I think that this question can not only change lives, but save them.

Bill O'Hanlon
Santa Fe, New Mexico
April 2004

Chapter One

Begin With a Miracle

Miracles happen to those who believe in them.
—*Bernard Berensen*

How would a miracle change your life? Would you get a better job, fix your marriage, stop drinking, keep your teenager home at night, make peace with your parents, silence your boss, bring back your deceased relative, or would it help you financially?

If you have tried therapy, traditional problem solving strategies or talked to a friend at length, and still find yourself haunted by the same problem and situation, The Miracle Question was written for you. In other words, if you have ever found yourself saying, "If only a miracle would happen…" this book will give you hope and direction. No matter what your issue or situation, The Miracle Question will give you a chance to begin achieving what you want and provide new options for living your life. It will do this for you because as soon as you stop thinking about why you *can't* have something and begin to look at how your life *could* be if a miracle were to happen, you will be on the road to solutions.

How can I make such promises? Because for over thirteen years, I have seen people change their lives when they answered The Miracle Question. They then realized that they had the power within themselves to make that miracle happen. Whether the issue was grief, sexual abuse, divorce, depression, anxiety, anger or addictive behavior, when my clients understood what was missing in their lives by answering the question, they were able to emotionally step out of their problems and begin finding a solution within themselves. They didn't need me to give them advice or tell them how to change things. They didn't even need other people or situations to change in order to try new experiences. They simply needed to answer The Miracle Question, learn from themselves how the answer to it would make a difference, and then realize that they were competent enough to achieve it.

The following scenarios are examples of how The Miracle Question "gave people their lives back". Each needed a miracle. Each was stumbling due to problems that seemed overwhelming.

The Couple

FELIX AND ELAINE: We need you to help us decide if we should get divorced or stay married. We've been married for nineteen years. We have three sons, aged six, eight and ten. We love each other, but the marriage just isn't working.

Felix and Elaine were a forty-something couple who came to me because they felt their marriage was deteriorating. They told me they had dated for eight years, first through high school and then college. Felix attended medical school while Elaine pursued a nursing degree. They were used to spending time apart, but once the kids arrived, they never seemed to have any time for each other at all. Coping with their careers and keeping up with the demanding schedules of three children was all-consuming. Neither was content in the marriage and both felt resentful about how their partner never made time for them. Was it worth it to stay together?

The Mother

PAM: My three-year-old son needs a heart transplant. If he doesn't have one, he'll die. I need help coping with this situation. I can't have any more children.

Pam cried throughout our session. Her son Malcolm had a rare type of tumor so enmeshed with his heart that it could not be removed. She and her husband, Alex, barely spoke these days. The fear of losing Malcolm had put a strain on both their marriage and careers. She was an engineer; her husband a salesman. Both were considering taking extended time off from their jobs to spend with

Malcolm. They were facing the last months of their child's life. How was Pam going to get through this?

The Professional Woman

SHEILA: I've had two abortions this year and now I'm pregnant again. I need to decide within the next week whether to abort this pregnancy.

Sheila was twenty-eight years old and in a casual relationship. She was successful in her career as a physical trainer. Although she was doing well financially, she was terrified to have a child on her own. She cared for Danny, the father of her child, but he cringed when she told him she was pregnant. She had a very loving and supportive family who would be there for her, but she had always envisaged having a child with someone who would provide the kind of home life that *her* family gave her. Her search for Mr. Right was leading her nowhere. Twice before she thought she had met the right person, someone who would provide her with that kind of life, but in both instances, it wasn't meant to be. Now she didn't know what to do.

The Professional Male

TERRY: I'm afraid I'm about to lose my marriage. I yell and curse at my wife all the time, even though I think she is the most wonderful woman in the world. I can't stop myself.

Terry was thirty-six years old and a successful attorney. During their six-year marriage, he and his wife Martha had accumulated money, a house and nice cars. They had one son. They also had a nightmare of a relationship; one he described as "a relationship just like my parents had". He had little guidance from his parents growing up, so he imagined that simply providing good things for those you loved was enough.

This seemed fine until Martha told him that it didn't even come *close* to being enough. He told me he'd already seen two therapists, but when both suggested anger management classes, he didn't return because he couldn't take time out of his schedule to attend the classes. In our sessions, he admitted that his mother was very abusive to him, hitting him and putting him down emotionally all through his childhood, especially after his father left. Whenever he wanted to see his dad, his mother put him down even more. Martha told Terry that unless he got help, she was going to divorce him. Terry felt like he had married his mother. How could he change things to save his marriage and not risk losing contact with his son?

Why I Changed My Approach as a Therapist

I have been a marriage and family therapist for twelve years. I've talked with families, couples, adults, children, and adolescents about all kinds of issues and experiences. Many people have come to me because they were desperate. For most, a better life depended on change—and fast. Some were sent by their spouse or physician. Maybe they were drinking, or they ate too much or too little. For some, their stress level was too high, or they were grieving the loss of someone important. Others came because someone else told them that they had a problem and needed professional help.

Before 1991, I would explore circumstances with my clients and help them figure out what they could do to change their lives. Sometimes the strategies worked, sometimes they didn't—but when they didn't, I always thought it was my client who wasn't cooperating. I regret this now, because I realize they were trying to tell me something, and I wasn't listening.

Not only wasn't I listening, I wasn't asking the right questions. I was asking questions I thought were necessary to gather information, understand their experiences, and gain insight into their dilemma. I gave advice because I thought it would be helpful and because that's what they were there for. I realize now that I never asked my clients to tell me how *they* really wanted things to be in their life. I didn't recognize that they had the power to create that possibility.

Now I know how to ask a different question. This is it:

"Suppose tonight while you sleep, a miracle happens. When you awake tomorrow morning, what will you see yourself doing, thinking, or believing about yourself that will tell you a miracle has happened in your life?"

To each of the clients featured in this chapter, I asked The Miracle Question because each person seemed to need just that—a miracle. I simply became their tour guide, showing them that they already had the answers they needed within themselves. I did not give advice. I did not suggest that they were in their situation because of historical baggage, nor did I give explanations on how that baggage would influence their life in the future unless they did things differently. As they told their stories, I just listened, focusing on their individual abilities, and helped them discover what they had overlooked when they realized their problems had clearly compromised their confidence.

Here's how it all worked out. Here are their answers to The Miracle Question.

The Couple

ELAINE: When we were first married, we were best friends. In our miracle we would be best friends again. We would be doing things we did then—dancing, hiking, talking, talking and more talking.

FELIX: The kids would be better behaved and we would share the responsibility for the kids more equally. Sometimes I think I have to do everything. In the miracle, she wouldn't get on the phone with her sisters at night and we would help the kids with their schoolwork together.

ELAINE: We wouldn't be so resentful and distrusting. Instead we would sit down and plan together for a change, like we used to.

FELIX: I think she's wonderful and I want her to want me again. In the miracle, she would look up from her book when I came home and be glad to see me.

Currently, the couple is re-creating their marriage based on how they began their relationship, and it's working. Because they're paying more attention to each other, their kids are behaving better. Now that they spend more time together, Felix feels he is becoming slightly more important to Elaine. She never knew that simply glancing up at him when he came in at night would mean so much. He had no idea that she still *would* like to go dancing like they used to. They both realized that they had similar, if not the same, goals.

The Mother

PAM: In the miracle, of course my answer would be that Malcolm would be well, but I have to be realistic. I suppose the next best thing would be that I would be able to be the best mom I can be while he is going through all of this, instead of just crying, which is all I can do right now because I am so stressed and afraid.

I asked Pam to tell me about ways she had coped during other times in her life when she felt stressed and afraid.

PAM: To be honest, I worked on the computer and did research. That distracts me from my problems and gets me focused.

I asked her how doing research on her son's condition might help her through the next few days.

PAM: I haven't really done that on my own yet, since I have talked to so many doctors. Maybe I can go online and see what I can find out.

Pam called me before our next appointment. She had done the research and located a surgeon who had experience with situations such as Malcolm's. After examining Malcolm's records, he referred her to a specialist in California. The whole family packed their bags. They went to Disneyland, and then met with a physician who saved Malcolm's life. The doctor removed the tumor. Today Malcolm is eight.

The Professional Woman

SHEILA: In the miracle I would be in a stable situation. I could raise my child as I was raised, with support from a loving partner and be financially secure.

I asked Sheila to think back over the past few years and describe instances when she felt stable and supported by outside sources.

SHEILA: I don't know. I'm not sure whether the father of this baby would be supportive. I know my family would. I still worry, though, whether I'm financially stable enough to do it on my own.

Sheila had supported herself for the past five years, and I commended her for this. I also mentioned that she was successful in setting goals for herself when she was employed and that she met those goals. We arranged to meet the following week, and I instructed her to watch for signs that the stability and support she craved were already in place.

She returned in a week to tell me her decision:

SHEILA: I am going to have the baby … I thought about what you said, you know, about maybe already having the stability and support in place, and I decided that I could do this on my own. Then I went to my parents who said I could live with them for now, and even after the baby was born if I need to. They were very supportive. They always have been. But the best part is, I told Danny I'm going to have the baby. He asked me to marry him. We're getting married in two weeks.

Danny and Sheila are now married and have two children.

The Professional Male

TERRY: Naturally, in the miracle, my wife and I would be getting along. I wouldn't be the jackass I am when I'm around her. She would know that I was trying. I think probably I would be a better dad, too.

I asked Terry how people at work would define his interactions with them, and how he works with clients and judges.

TERRY: I'm completely different at work. My secretary tells me I'm the best boss she's ever had. She's been my secretary for five years. My partners call me in on cases and ask me for advice with difficult clients because they say I have a way with words, particularly with clients who are demanding.

I asked him what he thought kept him calm at work.

TERRY: I try stepping into other people's shoes and thinking first, before I talk. In law school I learned how important it is to present myself professionally, and I work on that constantly.

I gave Terry an assignment. I asked him to think about being professional at home with his wife, as a husband and as a father. I mentioned that the mere fact that he came to talk about it, again, to someone new, told me that he probably valued his family's feelings about him more than his colleagues'. In other words, I asked him to do at home what he did at work.

TERRY: I never would have thought about it like that. I suppose I can do what I already do, I just never thought about doing it anywhere but the office.

After two months, Terry ended our visits. He and Martha were getting along very well and he was taking more time off to be with her and their son.

The Theory Behind The Miracle Question

This process, based on a model of therapy described as Solution Focused Therapy, has evolved in a novel manner. This different approach to solving problems doesn't require digging into past history and explaining *why* life has turned out the way it has. In many of the stories you have just read, the past was discussed briefly, but only as a way to better understand the person's abilities and resiliencies. The past is helpful only in regard to the client's ability to get through previous difficulties.

As I began using this approach, I looked at who my clients were, listened to their presenting problem and gave more time and attention to the talents they already possessed. They guided me to their own conclusions and solutions. They later told me that they left my office feeling empowered. They said they felt better, emotionally and physically, as if, finally, there was hope. They came back the next week having done something different in their lives. They noticed that people treated them better and, in return, they not only continued to make changes, but they were consistent with those changes. It is my belief that the changes they made were easier because they were developed by the client!

Several well-known psychologists were responsible for identifying the key ideas of the Solution Focused Therapy model. In the 1960s, Abraham Maslow decided that psychology had been moving in the wrong direction. Almost from the start, most psychological inquiries had explored and tried to understand the nature of emotional, behavioral and psychological pathology in human beings. Maslow believed that instead we should be studying the best, healthiest specimens of human beings to learn what we really want to know about people.

In 1966, The Mental Research Institute (MRI) in Palo Alto, California, started a brief therapy project. MRI therapists were convinced therapy could be accomplished in a much shorter time than the prevailing therapy standard by resolving the presenting problem rather than reorganizing families or developing insight. Jay Haley and Thomas Szasz believed it was best to treat people as if they were "normal", because when they are treated as normal they tend to act more normally.

Milton Erickson was convinced that individuals have a reservoir of wisdom learned and forgotten but still available. Humanistic psychology, Ericksonian, and systemic therapies all share a common emphasis on the importance of accessing client's resources and strengths, yet they differ from the Solution Focused Brief Therapy (SFBT) approach in significant ways. Unlike SFBT, these models emphasize the expertise of the therapist and they do not make the crucial distinction between solution development and problem solving and the resulting linguistic and practical differences and advantages therein. Nor do they include or encompass the work of the philosopher, Wittgenstein, which is a core ingredient of the SFBT approach. The actual provenance of the Miracle Question was first invented and used for solution development by Insoo Kim Berg in response to an extremely depressed woman who described a seemingly hopeless situation as "only a Miracle would help" (Berg and Dolan, 2001).

Steve deShazer, a well-known author and clinician, has said that it is the key that opens the door that matters most (in therapy), not the nature of the lock. In other words, analyzing and understanding the lock are unnecessary if one has a skeleton key that fits many different locks. Steve deShazer and Eve Lipchik were first to utilize the question in therapy.

As the model continued to evolve in the early 1980s, deShazer and his wife, Insoo Berg, founders of the Brief Family Therapy Center (BFTC) in Milwaukee, began asking clients what the therapists in their agency did that helped their lives to change. The clients told them that they had found their own resilience and competence through the conversations they had had with their therapists. Michelle Weiner-Davis, also at BFTC during that time, asked her clients what parts of their lives were better before the first therapy session. Their answers helped guide her therapy with her clients, because often, solutions had already occurred. Bill O'Hanlon took this a step further and began talking about possibilities rather than problems with his clients, thus offering opportunities for clients to heal from traumas such as sexual abuse by looking at themselves as survivors instead of victims.

Scott Miller of Chicago and Insoo Berg even went to the streets of Milwaukee and talked to skid row alcoholics, listening for signs of resiliency and working with them using this approach. Many of those people stopped drinking. The therapists only focused on *competencies*. Today, the solution-focused approach is an accepted model of therapy throughout the world. It has become attractive to managed care companies because therapists spend more time on goal setting and task development and less time on understanding the past. Solution Focused Therapy is not only brief, it is also effective.

Conclusion

I hope you find this book easy to understand and use as you seek your own solutions. I've tried my best to put aside psychobabble and simply talk about the possibility of bringing a miracle into your life. The process includes viewing life differently, focusing not on what causes your problems, but on the times when problems occur less. This can be as simple as:

- Recognizing that last night's argument over homework left your ten-year-old daughter sad and upset instead of motivated and productive. You were upset too. The night before, when you made popcorn and helped her with her reading, things went better.

- Glancing back over other tasks that your fourteen-year-old son has had to do in the past, and figuring out how he did them slightly better before, then thinking, "What did I do differently then?"

- Thinking back over the times when your marriage worked better and was more satisfying to you. Was it the time that you spent talking about positive things with your husband when he came home each night? What did he do that made you want to be close to him? What did he say that made the difference to your evening?

In the movie *Patch Adams*, Patch is a man who enters a problem-focused psychiatric hospital after he tries to kill himself. He meets many fellow patients but the one who intrigues him most is Arthur, a famous mathematician whom the techs say "counted too many fractions".

Arthur has a habit of walking around the hospital holding up four fingers and saying, "How many fingers do you see?" When other patients and techs tell him they see four fingers, he exclaims, "You're crazy." Patch is intrigued by the question, and late one night he talks to Arthur about it. Arthur holds his fingers up and asks Patch to tell him how many he sees. Patch says, "There are four fingers, Arthur." Arthur then pushes Patch to think differently when he says, "No, look at me. You are focusing on the problem. You can't see the solution if you focus on the problem. Look at me."

Blurring his eyes to see Arthur more clearly through his fingers, Patch's eyes see eight blurred fingers. Now when Arthur asks him, "How many do you see?" Patch tells him, "Eight." Thrilled, Arthur says, "Good, eight's a good answer... see what others fail to see out of fear and unconformity. See what no one else sees. You must see other things or you wouldn't have come here anyway. You must have seen something more than a bitter old man. I think you are on your way!"

The stories in this chapter are about real people who were looking everywhere for solutions except within themselves. They were so focused on trying to either avoid or understand their problems that they couldn't see a solution. This book will show you how to adapt the abilities you have in other areas of your life to your current dilemma. It will help you to open your eyes to solutions instead of focusing on the problem, thus freeing you to experience life as you have always wanted.

As I mentioned earlier, while explanations may define situations, they do *not* yield solutions. However, glancing back over the times when your life worked better will yield strategies to try *today*. Think of this process as one that first requires your looking forward to identify your miracle, then going backwards to note your abilities, and then to the present to implement your goal. You won't need to understand what's happened in the past that has *kept* you from being successful. Instead, you're going to identify what made you successful in the first place.

> To keep our faces toward change, and behave like free spirits
> in the presence of fate, is strength undefeatable.
> —*Helen Keller*

Chapter Two
Answer The Miracle Question

No one can go back and make a brand new start my friend,
but anyone can start from here and make a new end.
—Anonymous

Mark is a terrific hairdresser. One afternoon while cutting my hair, he seemed more enthusiastic than usual. Normally, he chats away about a recent trip or his dog. When I mentioned I was writing another book, he was intrigued. After I gave him a very brief explanation, he stopped, looked at me with surprise, and said, "This is too coincidental. You won't believe what happened to me yesterday."

He told me he had recently been feeling depressed and was trying to figure out what to do about it. On his way home from work the day before, he had driven by a billboard that advertised the Texas Lottery. The lottery jackpot was $29 million dollars. Like a lot of people, he said that he began fantasizing immediately about what he would do with $29 million dollars. He said it would definitely change his life and solve his problems, because with all that money, he could have more fun and feel less stressed about his job.

But then he told me something even better:

MARK: Something more remarkable happened as I drove past the sign. I started thinking to myself, you know, you could do some of that now, without the lottery. You could spend more time with your friends, get rid of some stress by trying a new activity and meet some new people. It wouldn't take $29 million to do that.

Mark didn't know it, but he was answering The Miracle Question.

When people think of a miracle changing their lives, they often forget to ask themselves, "How *will* $29 million dollars change my life?" Maybe you've often fantasized about it too. I know I have.

Maybe you have told yourself:

"I wouldn't have to work anymore."

"My family would live in a nicer home."

"Our kids would be able to go to college."

"I would travel around the world."

It sounds almost impossible, doesn't it, for those wishes to come true? Actually, it can even be depressing to think of all the things that you would be able to do if you had this good fortune. But hold that thought. Now take the next step and answer the next *very* important question:

"What would having my wish do for me?"

Your answers might read like these:

"If I didn't work, I would have more time at home. More time at home might mean I would have a better relationship with my family."

"If I had a nicer home, I would enjoy having people over more often. I would think of myself as more successful. That would give me confidence and I would probably be easier to be with at home."

"If I knew my kids could go to college, I might do more with them instead of scrimping and saving every cent for their education. I might spend less time worrying about money and take them on a vacation or do more activities with them now."

"If I could travel? Wow. I would get to see new things. I would feel more educated about the world and would be able to have better conversations with people. My kids and I could talk about the things we did together and develop a better relationship."

Notice how the goals went from impossible to possible? This process provides the opportunity for you to think about how *you* want things to be, and then helps you to explore some real possibilities. As you continue this chapter, you will be asked to focus on where you want to be, not on how you will get there. Walt Disney said: "If you can dream it, you can do it." (Remember, he started his empire with a mouse.)

Where is Your Cheese?

Speaking of mice, in *Who Moved My Cheese?* by Spencer Johnson, readers learn that sitting back, waiting for change, and questioning why it hasn't arrived for them doesn't work. Finding an alternate way through the maze and adapting to change does. The premise of this book is that finding alternative ways to do things will always cause things to turn out differently.

In his book, *Do One Thing Different*, Bill O'Hanlon says, "Insanity is doing the same thing over and over again and expecting different results." His book is full of tales about people who did something different and experienced a better result. He suggests some guidelines for changing how you think about your problem when you can't find *your* cheese. He encourages people to acknowledge their feelings and their past without letting them determine what they do. He suggests focusing on what they want in the future rather than on what they don't like in the present or the past. He also suggests challenging unhelpful beliefs about themselves and their situation, using a spiritual perspective to help them transcend their troubles and drawing on resources beyond their usual capabilities.

There's a good chance that life has been so unfair and such a struggle to you that you can't readily identify how you have dealt with problems successfully in the past. Sometimes when problems have taken over our lives, it's difficult to refocus and notice how we made it through, particularly when we see only the problems. That immobility or blindness to possibilities is what destroys our hope and keeps us stuck in depression, anxiety, anger, frustration and so on.

Begin thinking of the symptoms you have developed as reactions to a life that is not working for you. How have those symptoms interfered with how you want to live? To simply tell yourself that you need to get better so that you can get back to your old life is like expecting to fit your "round life into a square hole". It's destined to fail. Parts of your life must change for you to maintain healthy change yourself. To do that, you need to have a vision, confidence in your own abilities to achieve that vision, and a new set of actions. Your answer to The Miracle Question in the worksheets provided in this chapter will set your vision. This will provide you with a break from the way things are. It will provide the round hole in which to fit your round life. This is the process of The Miracle Question.

What About Your Significant Others?

Our conversation thus far has centered on you. Sometimes thinking solely of yourself can be frightening, particularly if there are significant others in your life who will most certainly be affected by your new ideas. Just thinking of how you want to live your life can be stifled by your responsibilities to others. In the next chapter we will discuss how you can accommodate the needs of others as you go through this process. You'd be set up for failure if we didn't discuss how others may react to you, so we will talk about it in a manner that will help you feel very comfortable. You won't put their needs aside, you will work *with* them. With this process, you'll pay attention to them more than you ever have and eventually you'll feel less resistance and more support because of how you will begin reacting to them. This will help to dissolve guilt that some of you may feel when you start making changes. It will be a respectful way to begin changing your life.

Until we get to that chapter, continue to concentrate on yourself, for only you know what your miracle needs to be. Allow yourself the luxury of imagining how a miracle will make a huge difference to your life.

Now Answer the Question

Let's start by seeing what happens when you answer The Miracle Question:

"Suppose tonight while you sleep, a miracle happens. When you awake tomorrow morning, what will you see yourself doing, thinking or believing about yourself that will tell you a miracle has happened in your life?"

Hold onto those thoughts! Write them all below. Dream…

_____

_____

_____

_____

_____

_____

Now that you've started to think about your miracle, let's examine the actions that you wrote and translate them into "miracle goals".

What are My Miracle Goals?

If you are like a lot of people, you might have let your imagination go wild when you answered The Miracle Question. I hope so. Chances are that your answers reflect the possibility that something very important is and has been missing from your life. It could be something you've never experienced yet feel you deserve, or something that you've lost and miss terribly. Whatever your heart's desire, it's acceptable, as long as it leads to a healthier and happier life for you.

Let's start slowly by examining what people have told me would compose their miracle and translate their statements into miracle goals, or what the miracle could do for you. This step will keep you grounded and realistic, yet open to your miracle.

"I will lose 50 pounds."

"I will get a promotion."

"I will not be depressed anymore."

"I will stay calm around my kids."

"I will stay sober."

"I will get divorced and find a better relationship."

These goals are important and honest. They're all great as a starting point for people who are describing their miracle. Achieving any of these goals will impact many areas of their lives, but bear in mind, all require a lot of quick change. They also require adjustments, possible uncomfortable situations and detailed explanations that often scare people away from taking the first step. That's why people often quit before the first goal is achieved.

Lasting change occurs more slowly and considers the *system* (a *system* refers to your family, marriage and job) within which you live. Obstacles in the form of expectations in relationships, job responsibilities or health issues can interfere with a person's motivation to keep focused only on goals. While goals such as those described above will lead to a better life, the chances of a person achieving these results immediately without any resistance or challenges are slim. This is how people get stuck and give up. The Miracle Question process is different.

Understanding the Miracle Goal

Let's look again at the goals previously mentioned and translate them into the new meanings the same clients gave me after I asked them to think about what the miracle would *do* for them. Notice how the original goals remain, but change slightly into more achievable goals that are much more specific, realistic and action-oriented.

I asked the clients: "What will it *do* for you when you begin achieving a small part of that miracle some day soon?"

- "When I lose 50 pounds, I will feel more attractive so I will probably socialize more. I would do some physical activities since it would be easier for me to move around."

- "When I get a promotion, I will get recognition for the work I have put in over the years, which I would find very satisfying. That would make me feel more confident. When I'm more confident, I might look forward to work. I might even take a risk once in a while and do something different for myself."

- "When I become happier, my wife will also be happier and we'll do some of the things that we used to enjoy together. It's been a long time since I felt like getting out. If I was not depressed, I would be going out much more often."

- "When I learn how to be calmer, my seventeen-year-old son and I will get along better. I might think we have a chance at some sort of relationship. I wouldn't be so angry all the time. Instead, I might smile occasionally. That would be a real switch. I'd be a lot nicer to be around. People would probably react better towards me."

- "When I'm sober and healthy again, I would be able to get up on weekends and do some sort of activity with the kids. I'd have energy. Everything would probably get a whole lot better at work because I would be more productive. I would have more money and my husband might be interested in spending time with me again."

- "In a different and safe relationship, I would make decisions for myself and follow through with them. I would think of myself more often rather than walking on eggshells. I would get a job outside the home and do things with my friends more often. I would be in a better mood."

Changing the Goals to Take New Actions

Let's take the first miracle goal through the process. It involves Sarah, whose alcohol abuse problem evolved into a goal for "health" rather than just quitting drinking.

SARAH: In my miracle I would stay sober.

LM: Great. What would being sober do for you?

SARAH: I would be healthier, I would keep a job and my family life would definitely improve. My kids would be proud of me.

After recognizing the physical and psychological difficulties of alcohol abuse and how overwhelming the task was to quit drinking, Sarah was able to think about how being sober would improve the quality of her life. Focusing simply on quitting drinking has troubled and challenged people for decades. People find it terrifying and often impossible when they think about giving up something that brings them relief, even if that relief has dangerous side effects and implications to their physical and mental health.

When confronted with that challenge, the problem drinker sees a life without drinking, not a life with anything different. This is a very difficult task to accomplish. No wonder it presents one of the toughest problems in mental health treatment. Yet, when the prospect of sobriety is allowed to color a picture more attractively in a person's life, with plenty of small achievements along the way, the goal becomes one of achieving something rather than leaving something behind. It becomes less of a life sacrifice and more of a life improvement.

LM: Tell me about the times when your family life was better, or you felt healthier and you had a job.

SARAH: There haven't been many good times since I began drinking five years ago. When I was living in Chicago things were better. I worked a lot and had to be accountable to my boss. I was promoted several years in a row, but I burned myself out by working too hard. After I quit the job, I spent more time at home with my kids while looking for a job. We got along better then too. Of course, when I finally found the last job, I had to give up time at home. I started traveling and I got lonely on the road. So once again I visited bars fairly often and it affected my work to the point that I was fired.

LM: So when you had a job where you had to be accountable fairly consistently, that helped. When you were at home with your kids and between jobs, you all got along. What does that tell you? What do you think worked before?

Sarah: Looks like I'm a person who needs a pretty structured job and life. I guess I could try to choose at least one day to visit my kids at their dad's house. They would probably like that. I've been so ashamed of my drinking that I've stayed away on purpose. I didn't think they would want to see me.

LM: What do you think the drinking did for you?

Sarah: Like I said, it began as a social thing when I was lonely. I suppose it also helped me relax. Actually, I thought I worked better after a few drinks. My productivity was up. It wasn't until I got fired that I realized it had gone too far.

LM: Finding a way to be more productive at work without drinking is important, as is helping you to relax and be in a social situation.

Sarah: Yes.

LM: Tell me about some times when you didn't drink as much when some of these things happened for you.

Sarah: There were times when I was first married and in a professional career that I didn't drink because I wanted to be on my toes. It was after the affair that things went downhill.

LM: What did you do then that helped you to stay focused on work and be social without drinking?

Sarah: I was very focused on my health then. I was a young woman, just out of college, no kids yet. I worked out and that relaxed me. I followed a list to stay structured in my job. I got promotion after promotion.

LM: You know, your miracle goal is within reach because you've done it before.

SARAH: I guess I have. I haven't thought about it that way.

LM: If we could step into the miracle you're describing for me, just for a week, what would your kids begin seeing that would make you feel proud?

SARAH: They would see a mom who is confident and has the energy to play softball with them again.

LM: Your job for the next week is simply to show them that. Let's talk about how you did that in the past and see how you can use the same thoughts and actions to begin achieving your goal.

Notice how Sarah's answers began to create a direction for her. Getting healthier, keeping a job and improving family life was slightly easier to think about and begin working on than getting sober, although it was obvious that sobriety was the main goal. Most important, she discovered that fact herself. I didn't tell her to quit drinking. Her drinking habit would have to change because activities that involve getting healthier would require less drinking.

Notice I said *less* drinking. Notice I also avoided a conversation about *alcoholism*. It would be ideal, of course, for her to stop drinking altogether, but many people who rely on drinking to survive are reluctant to do so. Improving job performance and family life might mean a shift in routine, again making drinking less of a priority.

The important point to remember in setting goals around The Miracle Question is to focus on what will be different, not what won't happen anymore. To say that she wants to stop drinking leaves Sarah with a direction that may be destined to fail unless she replaces the drinking with a productive action. That's why I asked her, "What did your drinking do for you?" To say that she wants to be healthier, have a better family life, and improve her job performance gives her another direction, and helps her to focus on several tasks to begin working on slowly. The Miracle Question should always be answered in terms of what is desired, not what is not wanted.

NOTE: It's important to note that by saying "drinking less" I am not saying that a problem drinker can continue drinking and still achieve lasting change in his life. If you or someone you love is so involved with alcohol that he is physically and emotionally hurting himself or endangering the lives of others, it is vital to contact a physician to work with that person and refer him for professional treatment. Perhaps this book will be helpful as an impetus for the person as he begins setting goals and making plans to rebuild his life. The treatment can then assist him in gaining freedom from a very dangerous habit. Chapter Eight contains more information on using The Miracle Question when dealing with harmful habits. If this is your concern, after reading Chapter Four, turn to Chapter Eight now for more specific ideas.

More Miracles Become Miracle Goals

The additional examples of miracle goals may be helpful as you figure out what your miracle will do for you in the next exercise:

I Miracle	II What the Miracle will do
I will win the lottery.	I will feel financially secure.
My spouse will give me attention.	I will feel loved.
I will stand up for myself.	I will feel important.
I will not be confused anymore.	I will make good decisions.
My wife will want to reconcile.	I will feel secure about myself.
I will get along with my parents.	I will feel supported and loved.
I will not be ill.	I will enjoy life better.
My husband would be alive.	I would feel content and less lonely.

Some of the miracles in the first column seem unrealistic—some are actually impossible—yet notice what happens in column two when people look for a broader meaning and ask themselves what the miracle will do for them. They become more realistic and possibility-oriented. With a more specific range of actions available in column two, the task becomes clearer. In Chapter Four, we will discuss how these new goals can then direct the Action Plan.

As you work through the following exercise, keep this process in mind. It is meant to guide you through the process to determine the meaning of your miracle, or your miracle goal. If you choose to do the process with someone, tell your confidant that you will need her support in brainstorming new ideas for your life but that you won't need her advice. Tell her you need her help in staying focused on what you want, not on what you don't want. This new way of thinking will change your response.

Miracle Actions

Define what your miracle answers (those you listed in the last exercise) will do for you when they begin happening.

_____

_____

_____

_____

Now that you've identified the changes you want your miracle to help you make, you have the necessary information to finally move yourself forward. You have taken the risk of dreaming of a better time and then taken the time to define what that dream will do for you. If defining the meaning of your miracle was difficult, read on. Many people struggle with The Miracle Question because their lives have been so downtrodden that depression and frustration have moved to the forefront. The following section will offer you an alternative to answering The Miracle Question.

By The Way … It's Okay to Struggle With the Question

We've focused on people who had the same thing in common: they were stuck because they thought either someone or something else was keeping them from their miracle. If you are struggling with a low perception of yourself and what you want, don't despair. It simply means that the problems, not you, are prohibiting you from imagining the person you want to be.

For example, looking back:

- Terry thought his mother was the culprit who damned him from having a healthy relationship with a woman.

- Sheila thought she needed the traditional "white picket fence" situation in order to successfully rear a child. Not having the perfect situation deterred her from making a decision.

Obviously, knowing what the problems were was not enough for either of these people to know what to change. It was always someone else's fault, some belief or other possible future situation that kept them from doing things the way they wanted. Their perception of themselves was dimly lit with possibilities, while their problems, anger and pain kept them further in that darkness. They needed a new perception of their miracle and only they knew what that would look like in their life.

Anna was such a client. This is her story.

The Client Who Couldn't Answer the Question

Anna had lost interest in talking to her husband about how unhappy she was. He told her to get out more and do some things for herself. "Hire a maid, just go shopping," he told her. Depressed, she was contemplating divorce. How could he be so cold-hearted? After I asked her The Miracle Question, Anna told me she was so down she couldn't even imagine a better day, much less answer the question. I wasn't surprised.

While Anna told me about her life, I listened for the abilities that would describe how she had coped during other difficult times. I soon learned that she was both competent and resilient. She emerged from a very unhappy childhood in which she was constantly criticized by her parents and moved out of her house at seventeen. After a few difficult relationships, she met her current husband, who was attracted by her independence. She talked about her two young children fondly, bragged about their successful school life and even remarked how well her husband had built up their home business over the years. The fact that she was still able to take care of her kids, perform daily routines and not be totally consumed by her sadness meant that she could try to think of a different answer.

LM: As you go through the next week, I want you to watch for any time, place and situation when you feel a little less sad. You'll really have to watch closely! It could be happening at any time. It will help if you write down your discoveries. I look forward to hearing what you discovered when you return in a week.

Anna returned a week later to tell me about a day that she had spent volunteering at her daughter's elementary school.

ANNA: Something happened last week that was kind of … good. I spent an afternoon serving lunch at a PTA meeting as a volunteer. I usually do accounting for our business at home so I really don't socialize much. After the lunch I thought about how much I enjoyed doing that. I even thought about calling the school again to find out whether they needed more help from me this week. I realized then that I needed to be a part of something. (Smiling) I felt like I had something in common with those women. I never thought I'd enjoy that so much.

During the next school year, Anna was the PTA's hospitality chair. She liked the position because it required her attendance at the monthly meetings and didn't detract from the time required for her home business. These new activities were just enough to form some new friendships and give Anna's social life a needed boost.

Anna told me her husband seemed impressed by her new position and it pleased her that he noticed. During their time alone, she found that she had more to talk to him about. Since their discussions focused on topics other than housework, business or kids, he seemed more interested. In fact, since she began volunteering more at school, she started feeling less angry with her husband.

Anna didn't have to divorce her husband to make the changes in her life that she felt she needed. When she was faced with answering The Miracle Question with a short-term goal for satisfaction, she watched for the change and became aware of the times when she felt better. Discovering her miracle, she began to focus on what she needed to do differently, stopped blaming her husband and took new actions for herself. She remained responsible to her family while becoming responsible for her own happiness. Let's look at how her process unfolded:

The Miracle Question Process

Anna's Miracle: Anna noticed that if she were to affect a miracle, it would involve her enjoying social contact while contributing something worthwhile, particularly at her daughter's school. She said that she enjoyed meeting up with other women and loved feeling as if she had a purpose.

The Miracle Goal: Anna felt important when she belonged to a group of people with similar interests. She liked the school atmosphere. She wanted to contribute and had a need to feel as though she was making a difference.

The Exceptions: Anna was a strong, competent individual who had endured an unhappy childhood, absent of guidance, yet was able to move out and support herself independently while still a teenager. She was also able to function at home as a mother and wife even when depressed. She had the skills to set herself a goal and move toward it independently.

The Action Plan: Anna would add social time to her week on a regular basis, which would give her regular contact with other adult women, preferably at her daughter's school, where she felt she was contributing something important.

The Result: Anna volunteered on a weekly basis and ran for a PTA office that had particular significance to her. Feeling better about herself, she and her husband had more to talk about and she was less dependent on him to feel valued. He, in turn, was impressed by her new actions and validated her efforts.

An Alternative Miracle Question Exercise

If you couldn't think of an answer to your Miracle Question at the beginning of this chapter, try the following steps that will help you to answer it later:

1. As you go through the next (day or week), watch for times when things are slightly better. Write a description of those times below:

    _____

    _____

    _____

2. What activities or interactions brought you some satisfaction? Write them below:

    _____

    _____

    _____

3. What did those activities or interactions do for you as you experienced them? Write how you felt and what thoughts occurred during those activities.

    _____

    _____

    _____

    _____

4. How will your life be when you start adding more of these experiences on a regular basis?

    _____

    _____

    _____

    _____

This process utilizes the same concept behind the Miracle Question and is another way to identify the components of your miracle. After Anna's story, you read about how the process worked. A brief explanation of the actual process is:

1. **The Miracle**: The answer to the Miracle Question.

2. **The Miracle Goal**: How the answer to the question will affect a person's life.

3. **The Exceptions**: A description of the times when the goal happened slightly more often and the problems happened less often.

4. **The Action Plan:** The plans that developed from examining the goal and the exceptions.

5. **The Results:** What changed and how the task worked to accomplish the changes.

You Can Even Help Others Define Their Miracle

Can you imagine this? It's possible. You probably know people who complain and do little to change things. Confronting others rarely works because it's offensive and disrespectful and when people feel this way, they become resistant to change. Instead, let's focus on how we can help people think of how they *want* things to be rather than complain about what they *don't want.*

Try thinking differently about those who complain. View them as people who are stuck rather than people who grumble about everything. For some people, it's easier to complain than act. Look around your workplace, observe your home environment, listen to your family discussions and participate in your community. Pay attention to the people who constantly complain without offering to change anything. Some people swear that by complaining they clear the air and get things off their chest, but where do those complaints eventually go? Nowhere. When their audience goes home and there is no one left to listen to them, what do they do to change things? You know the answer. Do something different the next time you have a conversation with them. As you view them as stuck, without new direction, talk with them differently:

"That sounds just awful. I really don't know how you've handled this so far. How would you rather things be?"

They may look startled or annoyed, and tell you, "I don't want this, I don't want that." But stay calm, kind, and say:

"I don't blame you. What do you want instead?"

Keep prodding if you like, containing your frustrations, (smiling to yourself) until you get the person to tell you something he *really* wants. It may take time, but eventually he'll begin to realize he's complaining to someone who doesn't want to hear his complaints. If he can't tell you what he wants, ask him to think about what he would like to be different and set a time to meet and discuss it together. This will be good training for you too, particularly on the days when *you* want to complain. You can use this technique with children, teenagers or adults. In fact, the younger the person, the better the chance she will know what she wants. Try it at your next staff meeting and watch some people scratch their heads while others nod, smile and thank you for the break. It will make for a more productive meeting.

Conclusion

You have now answered The Miracle Question and defined your miracle goal. I hope you will relax and now begin recognizing times when these identified actions happen. Chances are that if you have defined them as your miracle, you have experienced them once or twice in another situation or you wouldn't want them again. The next chapter will help you to learn more about identifying those better times and then achieving them. You will do this by identifying your "exceptions".

> We are the hero of our own story.
> —*Mary McCarthy*

Chapter Three
Check Out Your Exceptions

What we see depends mainly on what we look for.
—John Lubbock

What's gone better for you today?

As you look back over the past day or two, or even the last evening, think of a few things that went better for you. With the new thoughts about your miracle and the hope it creates, I would wager something went better, even if it was only slightly better. Write about anything that's gone better below:

_____

_____

_____

Who noticed what went better or remarked that you seemed slightly better?

_____

If nobody noticed or said anything, write what they should have noticed about you below:

_____

_____

_____

_____

The answers you wrote are called "exceptions". Exceptions are simply times when life works better, or times when problems are less likely to take over. In this chapter you will take on the task of identifying times when life has worked slightly better for you. You will work on identifying your exceptions in the exercises. You will use your miracle goal and miracle answer to search for times when those goals were more likely to happen in the past. Your exceptions will guide you toward attaining your goals again and again. You will also identify the exceptions of the people in your system.

It's Not Easy Being Exceptional—But You Can *Be*

Therapist Michael White once shared the following thought:

> Life is like a road. It seems as if boulders are placed in front of us constantly as we go through our lives. We get past one boulder and then there's another. It can get pretty discouraging. Each time we wonder how we will ever get around the next one. Yet, all we have to do is to look behind us at all of the other boulders that we have passed successfully along the same road.

In identifying your exceptions, remember that exceptions are the times when you are able to deal with problems in a way that makes them less burdensome for you. They are also the tools that will help you to achieve the life you want. For example, as you begin identifying the times when people are the most cooperative and adaptive at work, you may learn that it was how you approached them that made the difference. When you identify ways you have been successful in relationships at home, you may find exceptions that surprise you but made a difference to your loved ones. Whether the exceptions are discoveries you make or others describe to you, they are the keys to success.

Some people have difficulty identifying exceptions because they stay so focused on their problems. If you still doubt you've ever been successful, or that you even have exceptions, look over the following statements. They are common, yet they were, for the most part, untrue after they were explored further. Under each statement, I have added exception-stimulating questions that helped people realize they'd been more successful in their lives than they thought. They also realized that things really had not been as bad as they had perceived them to be. Try to identify a situation similar to yours and consider the questions underneath the statements.

"I'm always depressed. I think I've been depressed all my life."

LM: Please explain, then, how you've been able to complete your college degree, get married, have a child and stay with a job that you don't particularly enjoy. How have you managed all this while being depressed? What does that say about the kind of person you obviously are?

"I've never been successful at any job."

LM: Could you tell me, then, how you have been able to keep your current job for over two years? What other jobs have you had for at least six months? How would you say you were able to keep those jobs? What would your colleagues or your boss say about you? And tell me about times when you felt just slightly successful.

"I've never been able to commit to a relationship… something is wrong with me."

LM: You've told me how you stay in touch with friends from high school and attend your high school reunion every few years. You also have told me how you volunteer at the church and manage to stay close to your six-year-old daughter even though you and your wife are divorced. What's your secret to staying committed to those relationships?

"I always blow up and say things to my daughter that I regret later. I never can control my anger."

LM: As we were talking, I learned that you have a very stressful job. You said you've been a secretary for five years. You also told me that each day you feel so stressed at work that when you get home you just blow up. How would you explain your ability to stay calm at work for over eight hours a day?

"Life is always stressful for me. I can't get anything accomplished, ever!"

LM: As the mother of four children, two of whom are twins, I'm amazed that you had the time to talk to me. You said you have a babysitter whom you call when you just can't take it anymore. How do you always know to do that? How did you accomplish coming to our meeting today?

"My son is sixteen and a junior in high school. I have a fear that moving here was a bad idea and that he won't graduate since he seems so stressed. We've moved over three times during his childhood and I am feeling really guilty about that."

LM: How has your son been able to stay on track with his school work so far? How has he been able to do well in school when he has encountered busy or difficult times in the past? During the other times you moved, how did he adapt? What would he say you could do to help him be less stressed now?

"My husband and I have been married for fifteen years. We fight all the time. I can't remember a time when we didn't fight. I can't take it anymore."

LM: Take me back to a time when you were first attracted to each other. What made you want to marry him? How have you been able to stay together in spite of the fighting for over fifteen years? Tell me about the times when you do fight and then settle it.

"My father is too possessive. I'm twenty-six years old and I live on my own. You would think I was six years old by the way he's always telling me how to live my life. I don't want to be cruel to him because he's older now, but I really want him to see me as an adult."

LM: How were you able to move out on your own and know that you have your own life? How have you been able to communicate what you need from your dad in the past, in reference to other situations? Tell me about the times when your father "almost" saw you as an adult and treated you like one. What do you do in other relationships in which people see you as an adult?

When I focused on the *exceptions* in the statements instead of trying to understand the *reasons why* people couldn't be successful, suddenly there were *other* thoughts to consider, other instances to evaluate. When considering exceptions, it's as if a new bag of tricks is placed in front of you and anything in it is yours for the taking. Out of these considerations come new ideas for tasks, and new tasks lead to new results. That's how change happens.

Never Say Never and Always Ignore Always

It's important to eliminate words like "never" and "always" from your vocabulary. They're responsible for two of the most common traps that keep people stuck in unhappy situations. "Never" and "always" leave no room for hope and possibility. Besides, no one is angry twenty-four hours a day, seven days a week. People are rarely depressed all day long, seven days a week, particularly if they perform the responsibilities required of having a family or a job. There have to be times when a person keeps going despite his emotional state.

If your perception is that things *always* happen to you and that you *never* get a break, you are depriving yourself of information that could open your door to new solutions. Mere thoughts can be that powerful! The Miracle Question process is designed to change your thoughts from what you can't do to what you can do or have done. For one day, listen to the number of times certain people use the words "never" and "always". Ask yourself how happy and productive they are. They are probably not very happy, often choosing to complain rather than act. Don't let yourself be part of that crowd anymore.

Exercise 3.1: Find the Exceptions

Let's start by looking at your current exceptions:

Describe times recently when your life went better at home. What did you do with your child, spouse, partner or alone that made things better for you? For everyone?

_____

_____

_____

_____

_____

_____

_____

What did you do at work last week that made things just slightly better for you? What would your boss or supervisor say you did?

_____

_____

_____

What healthy activities did you engage in recently that made you feel better?

_____

_____

_____

What was one thing you did that helped you to have a better evening last night?

_____

_____

_____

What would your partner/spouse say you did recently that made your relationship more enjoyable?

_____

_____

_____

Don't be surprised if you find yourself struggling with these questions. At first it's hard to recognize exceptions. Most of us can pinpoint what didn't work yesterday because those problems *interfered* with our routine. But when you consider that each day contains twenty-four hours and each week consists of one hundred and sixty-eight hours, it makes sense to note that problems don't occur all the time.

Thus, exceptions occur when the problems do not. That's what this exercise is asking you to do. From now on, become acutely aware of times when problems are not as prevalent in your life. It may be as specific and simple as identifying certain times of the day. Wonder to yourself, "What went better this morning, this afternoon, this evening?" Maybe you and your daughter chatted on the way to school and she wasn't as abrupt as she normally is. What did you do differently? What would she say you did differently? Begin learning to make a mental note of the situation, place or the people involved and, most importantly, what you did and thought about as you experienced those actions.

Remember: Don't do Anything New

As you work through the Miracle Question process, it's important to avoid taking on new actions. In other words, don't attempt anything unless you have had success doing something similar before.

When you look at how you've accomplished other feats and changed your behaviors, you can get a hint of what you could do now. Those aren't new behaviors—they're successful ones. The tough part is looking at how you did them instead of what you didn't do.

For example, I worked with George, a gambler who saw his "addiction" to gambling as a new problem. His marriage was in jeopardy. When he told me about how he quit using cocaine ten years ago, it gave me clues that he knew how to beat this new habit. After we talked about the similarities between the two problems he was able to figure out what he needed to do. While attempting to quit his cocaine habit, George distanced himself through admitting himself to a treatment center. Afterwards, he envisaged all the people in his life who had died of drug use in a casket. From that information, we talked about distancing himself from his paycheck, which he cashed each Friday so he could gamble at the racetrack. He decided he should have it automatically deposited instead of handed to him each week.

I suggested George think about his marriage in a casket as he left work on Friday with his next paycheck. This immediately brought him to tears. I worried slightly because I knew the direct deposit set-up would take time. But I worried for nothing—George took it upon himself to immediately lock his paycheck in his glove compartment on Friday afternoon, and there it stayed. He didn't return to the track again, and is still married.

Exercise 3.2: Match Your Actions with Exceptions

The following questions do not ask you to identify problem-free times. Instead, they ask you to consider times when the problems occurred slightly less or not as often. For most people, there have been times when things went smoother, but they didn't recognize those times as such because they were so glad that things were better. Nonetheless, those times reveal very important exceptions worth noting and examining. Consider all kinds of circumstances when you have come close to achieving the same type of goal you have named. Go outside the context of your current miracle and look at other areas of your life.

You may be a terrific secretary known for her patience. Yet when you come home at night, your thirteen-year-old daughter brings out the worst in you. How do you cope with irate customers all day long? What do you tell yourself? If you were to use those abilities with your daughter tonight, what would be different? The way you handle things at work is an example of an exception. The frustrations are similar, yet you handle them differently in two different contexts. But the skill is the same.

What Your Miracle Will Do for You

Write the "miracle goals" (what your miracle will do for you) you described in Chapter Two below. Then identify the exceptions that match those goals in the next few questions.

_____

_____

_____

_____

_____

_____

_____

_____

_____

_____

Describe a time when your miracle goals nearly happened for you in similar or other circumstances.

By looking into the dynamics of varied situations in our lives and learning what keeps us focused and behaving as we really want, we define strategies that can help us with current dilemmas. Often, we can't see those strategies but others can. Once those strategies are identified, you know what to do in a crisis situation. Instead of staying upset, consider this question: "How have I handled tough situations like this before and survived?" This immediately helps you define some strategies to use and calms you down because you have something effective to do.

_____

_____

_____

_____

_____

_____

_____

_____

_____

What did you think or believe about yourself that helped the exceptions to occur? Where were you? Who was with or not with you? What was different in any way?

_____

_____

_____

_____

_____

_____

_____

_____

_____

_____

How would others describe how you have accomplished the above exceptions? What qualities, assets and abilities would they say you have that helped you to accomplish them?

_____

_____

_____

_____

_____

_____

_____

In the last exercise you listed exceptions that will become your strategies for your Action Plan in Chapter Four. As you continue reading the next story, you may identify with some of the feelings and exceptions Carla discovers about herself. If so, go back and add more exceptions to the previous exercise. These exercises are only the beginning. As you begin to look at your life differently, you will discover more exceptions.

Adopting a Life Without Depression

In the following case, exception-stimulating questions motivated Carla, a woman whose depression and chronic fatigue had left her with no hope at all. As you read the passage, watch for Carla's exceptions.

Carla came to me because she had been diagnosed with Chronic Fatigue Syndrome (CFS) and her physician felt that talking to someone might help her to cope with being so depressed. For four years she had worked at a job she disliked immensely. To make things worse, her parents disapproved of her chosen lifestyle—she was living with Jan, a partner whom she loved—and she wanted them to accept her decision. Carla had visited several different physicians, including a physician who specialized in family therapy, searching for answers to her depression. He prescribed an antidepressant, yet Carla improved only slightly. Eventually, she went on disability, claiming that she barely had enough energy to get out of bed. Even though she got more rest, she still felt very depressed and exhausted, as if her life had no direction. I asked Carla The Miracle Question. She responded thoughtfully:

CARLA: In the miracle, I'd quit my job. You just don't know how much I dread going each day. It's not that I don't want to work; I would much rather be working in a different field, one that's creative and fun. I would also be less depressed, more energetic and be doing things I want to do for a change. I have always tried to please other people. Also, my parents would accept Jan as someone I love instead of ignoring the fact that we are together.

LM: Tell me about the times when you feel less depressed and less worried about your parents' opinion.

CARLA: When I visit my niece and nephew things are good. I love children and I love watching my mother and the grandchildren together. I feel like we're a family and the depression subsides a bit. Sometimes I take the kids for a week, and although we're always on the go, I rarely feel tired when I'm with them.

LM: What does having your niece and nephew around do for you?

CARLA: I feel fulfilled. I would love to have my own child. I've thought about adopting a baby, but I'm not really sure what Jan thinks about it. It's one of those subjects I've hinted at but she hasn't responded. I know I need to face the possibility of not having children, but it just makes me so sad.

Carla's response was important because she described three things that would make a difference in her life—working at a more satisfying job, having her parents accept Jan, and caring for a baby. Her need to care for a baby and have a family with Jan seemed enormous.

LM: In the miracle, you would not be working and you would have a baby. What would that do for you?

CARLA: I would feel loved, important, as if I were fulfilling a need I've been trying to satisfy all my life. I love kids.

LM: Where else in your life do you feel loved, important and slightly happier, as if your life were fulfilling?

CARLA: I work at the church nursery on Sunday mornings. In one way, that's the toughest time for me, but it's also the highlight of my week. I'm always going to a toy store and wandering through the aisles looking at books, toys and other things for kids. I've even thought about working in a store like that but I am so tired from this illness that I can't imagine going through an eight-hour day working for someone else.

LM: When you are around kids and things that remind you of kids, you're happier. I'm going to ask you to do something different just for the next week. I'm not sure how you will do this, but I would like you to do something that relates to being around kids a little more often. When you began talking to me about children, you smiled for the first time in our conversation. I have a feeling this is what's been missing.

CARLA: I think so too. I guess I'd decided that it was something I couldn't have.

LM: Over the next week, choose a day or two and pretend that the miracle has happened. Live it however you like.

Carla returned the next week and told me she and Jan had contacted an adoption agency. They had both put off the idea of adopting until Carla told Jan about our conversation. She also told me that she'd decided to start a business selling children's books and other items through the Internet. She'd always enjoyed going to flea markets looking at children's items and had worked at a bookstore when she was a teenager. She looked back at her life and found many times when working with children, including her nephew and niece, had brought her the most joy.

Today, Carla and Jan's son Adam is four years old. Carla runs a successful mail-order business, which allows her to stay at home with Adam. Jan is as delighted with their son as she is. Carla takes him on her road trips to festivals and reports that she feels energized and happier than she can remember. Her parents are more accepting of Jan since they see the bond she has with their grandson.

If you noticed, the words that helped Carla were those that focused on what would make things better rather than what would not be happening in her life. Asking about why things happen to us and discussing what is wrong in our lives rarely gives us any direction. Instead, it makes us relive the doom and gloom of the present and literally suffocate our dreams. It's better to look for times when we are achieving what we want, even if it's on a small scale.

Carla's Miracle: More energy, a new job, doing something creative and fun.

The Miracle Goal: A feeling of fulfillment.

The Exceptions: When working with children in the nursery or visiting with her niece and nephew, Carla felt energized and happier.

The Action Plan: Begin the process of adopting a baby. Quit the current job. Plan an exciting and more fulfilling business.

The Result: Carla and Jan are the happy parents of a young boy. Carla runs a successful Web site and Jan is content working outside the home. Carla is energetic and hasn't experienced any CFS symptoms since the adoption, except for the normal fatigue from very busy and very happy days. The couple is planning to adopt another child.

Consider Your System Before Moving Forward

Remember how we discussed the importance of considering your significant others? Now we will. It's imperative to consider your *system* as you prepare your Action Plan. Your system involves your significant others and anyone else with whom you interact on a fairly regular basis. Your system may involve your current partner or spouse, family of origin (parents, step-parents or adoptive parents), children, employer and colleagues at work, and friends and acquaintances. Why is identifying your system so important? If you have ever played with dominos and lined them up next to each other in a row, you know how pushing just one can result in all of the dominos falling down.

The same goes for your system. If you operate the same way on a day-to-day basis, your system will react to you in the same manner. Imagine what will happen when you begin to do things differently. Will your system react? Of course it will. The roles of everyone involved will change. This can make people uncomfortable, especially if their comfort or needs depend on you. By determining the people who will support you most, you will deter any possibility of failure by gathering their support as you move forward. This careful planning and consideration of others will help you to make changes and enable you to follow through. There will be fewer surprises and more chances for success.

Exercise 3.3: Understanding the Values and Needs of Your System

The following exercise is designed to help you to learn the steps necessary to make change tolerable for people in your system. This will improve your chances of following through with your new goals. As you complete the following exercise, consider the people who will be affected most by the new changes in your life. Include those who will be there to applaud your progress and those who might not feel positive about your change. If you have always considered other people first, trust your abilities to know how to deal with your system, because this is what you have always done.

1. What would your family, friends and spouse or partner say they depend on you for the most?

Family

_____

_____

_____

_____

Friends

_____

_____

_____

_____

Spouse or Partner

_____

_____

_____

_____

_____

2. Think of some other small changes your system has made successfully in the past. What assets and beliefs seemed to help the people in your system adapt to those changes, even if those changes were difficult for them?

Family

_____

_____

_____

_____

_____

Friends

_____

_____

_____

_____

_____

Spouse or Partner

_____

_____

_____

_____

What assets/abilities does your spouse or partner have that will help him or her cope?

Spouse or Partner

_____

_____

_____

_____

3. What would your family, friends, spouse or partner say they wanted you to achieve, succeed at or accomplish in your life?

_____

_____

_____

_____

_____

(If you are not employed, skip the next two questions, or substitute another part of your system for the word "employer" such as teacher, clergyperson or the like.)

4. What would your current employer say he/she values in you most?

_____

_____

_____

_____

_____

5. What would your employer support your doing differently in your life or your job? What has he/she said or done in the past that assures you of this? (If this is a tough question to answer because of a difficult boss, consider what you will need to do to accommodate his/her needs as you make changes.)

_____

_____

_____

_____

_____

Remember, systems can be resistant because those involved will have to adjust to your changes. Some may resist adjusting. Realizing that this may occur, your plans may change, but you don't have to abandon them altogether. Cooperate with yourself and just go slower. You may have to reevaluate parts of relationships that benefit you. If a particular relationship still works for you, great; if not, perhaps it's time to do something different with it. Recognize that everyone has his or her own agenda. It's much more respectful to believe in someone's ability to handle a "different" you than it is for you to stay the same so that his life isn't interrupted.

Exercise 3.4: Step Up to the Scale

This exercise will help you identify how your system reacts to change. It will also help you develop a strategy for your new actions. Think of the people with whom you are intimately, professionally and biologically involved on an everyday basis. Write their names below, and next to each name, give the person a number based on how much support you need from him/her:

I strongly encourage you to take extra care and time with any person with a "5" or higher rating, because you will need to be prepared for the responses you receive. In other words, not only are you looking at your strengths in this process, you are looking at the strengths and resiliency of those important persons as well. The answers you uncover will help you ease into change with minimal inconvenience to yourself and others. You'll be more motivated because you'll be prepared for reactions. The next section will help this happen.

Before You Change Yourself...

If you have close relationships with your family or significant others, chances are you know what makes them uncomfortable with something you do. But have you identified how they adapt to those changes? When my daughter Kelli was in high school, she was head cheerleader and often came home with frustrations about her sponsor or the other girls on the squad. She would stomp in, say hello under her breath and retreat to her room. It was my occupational hazard at first to try to talk to her about what was bothering her. I learned quickly that she didn't see this as a solution. I learned to let her be, and later, when she was ready to talk, she did—or didn't. Typically, it took a couple of hours for her to emerge in a better mood. I changed my approach of "wanting to talk about it" to "I'll wait until she's ready". This helped us get through some turbulent years. She is now in college and we still have a great relationship.

Consider sitting down with the significant people in your life and telling them that you are planning some changes. Tell them that you're also concerned about what they might need from you in the process. Their answers will help you plan. If this makes you nervous, that's normal. It's one thing to think about what a person might say, but quite another to ask him. But consider this: If someone close to me told me this, I would be impressed with her respect for me. It would tell me that I was important to her and that she was important to me, too.

You will raise your self-respect when you let other people know what's important to you. However, you may also know people who will argue with you or confront you about your need for change. You may want to consider this before confiding in them, and you may resolve to simply move forward without informing them, if that works best for you, and perhaps for them too. Think back to a time when you made a small change. Did someone rebel but later adapt? Perhaps those close to you will benefit from ideas similar to the following:

- Forewarn your wife that you're going to make some changes in your life. Tell her those changes do not mean that she is any less important to you. Tell her that in fact, she is very important and you need her support. Ask her what she needs from you. Tell her what you need from her.

- Tell your children that even though you're taking a job that will take time away from them, you're also going to set times when you are home to play and do activities with them. Ask them what activities they would like to do with you. Tell them what it will mean to you to have their support.

- Tell your husband you may begin doing things for yourself slightly more often instead of being at the beck and call of everyone in the family. Assure him that your doing so does not mean he is less important to you. Ask him to think about things he would like to do with you on a routine basis. Tell him about the activities you would love to do with him.

- Tell your grandchildren that while you love to have them for the whole weekend, you need some time to relax after a busy week. Ask them to tell you different days that they would like to come over so you can all enjoy your time together. Tell them their support will help you to relax further.

- Tell your teenage daughter that you know getting home late from her job puts her on a different time schedule than yours, but you need less noise at midnight. Ask her to think of something else she can do when she comes home late that would help her relax. Tell her what you're willing to do when she complies.

- Tell your son that his extracurricular activities have become too much work for both of you. Then ask him to name two or three activities that you can both agree on. Tell him how his understanding will make you excited to do whatever you can to make them happen.

- Tell your colleague at work you understand that she's been under stress and has depended on you for help, but that you are now ready to focus on your own work. Then ask her how else she will cope with her own responsibilities, and be supportive. Give her a timeline when you will no longer be able to assist her.

- Tell your husband that you're not happy with your job and that you want to return to school to finish your degree. Ask him to tell you what you can do to make this transition better for him and your two small children. Tell him what you need from him.

Notice how each scenario included:

(a) What you feel and need to do differently.
(b) Asking the significant other what he/she will need from you as you begin the process.
(c) Telling the significant other what you will need from him/her.

Some of your significant others may doubt your reasons for needing to change. They may question or accuse you of foolishness. Trust that when they see you happier, they will respect what you are doing. In fact, think about other people they respect and think of others who asserted themselves to your significant others and gained their respect. Even if they're people who simply want to keep you in the same situation because it's easier for them, recognize that not changing for their benefit will forever keep you from your own happiness. Trust that they will survive and do all you can to accommodate their needs. Then look toward others who will give you support. Cherish the friends who would cheer you on toward a better life. Keep them in mind as you begin to make small changes.

Exercise 3.5: The "Fives" Have It

Planning miracle strategies with your system in mind will lessen the chance that your plan will fail. It would be easy to tell you, "Just do it and let everyone deal with it." But who would catch the fall out? You would. Besides, if that strategy worked, you wouldn't need The

Miracle Question today. Your compassion and concern for others will help you move forward, by caring for people in your system. Don't allow those traits to lead you off track for someone else's peace of mind. Do your best to consider the feelings and needs of those important to you. Considering others is humane and respectful. It's what keeps us in relationships. You can have both. You just have to recognize how the plan will work best for everyone and then take the tiny steps toward your miracle, slowly. The next exercise will assist you in planning your steps.

Write your answers below for those members of your system who received a "5" and higher in the last exercise:

How long has it taken the significant people in your life ("5" and higher) to adapt to changes you have attempted in the past? What would they say you did to help the process?

Name: _____

How this person adapts to change: _____

_____

_____

Name: _____

How this person adapts to change: _____

_____

_____

Name: _____

How this person adapts to change: _____

_____

_____

Name: _____

How this person adapts to change: _____

_____

_____

Getting Better All the Time

Make a promise to yourself to look for exceptions every day. Before you fall asleep, think about what worked for you that day. Look beyond the problem and what did not work and focus, focus, focus on what did. It may be as simple or as small as thinking fondly about your infant daughter after an irate colleague confronted you. This simple thought helped calm you. Thinking about the vacation you are going to take in a month may have helped you dig into the next mound of paperwork. It could be the way your wife distracted your toddler son while you dressed this morning and allowed you to have a conversation with your older daughter. It could even have been the photo on your desk or kind word from a colleague that gave you a moment of joy during your current sadness.

Whatever they are, your exceptions will always be the answer during frustrating times. Use the last chapter in this book as a journal. There are words to get you started in the first few pages. It will serve as a scrapbook for your daily exceptions and actions. Then, on days when life's interferences get in the way, refer to your journal for support and be instantly revitalized by what you have already written.

Conclusion

The purpose of this chapter has been to help you to begin noticing your exceptions, identifying how your system will react as you begin changing, and realizing the times when your miracle is happening more often. You're now changing your focus and your perception toward solutions, not problems. You're escaping from the influence and intrusion of the troubles in your life. Because of this, your strategies for solving problems will be unique to you. They will develop in the next chapter as we focus on the Action Plan. Until now, other people have given you advice. Now it's time for you to advise yourself.

> Happiness is a state of mind.
> It's all according to how you look at things.
> —*Walt Disney*

Chapter Four

Write Your Action Plan for Change

Life is made of moments, small pieces of glittering mica in a long stretch of gray cement. It would be wonderful if they came to us unsummoned, but particularly in lives as busy as the ones most of us lead now, that won't happen. We have to teach ourselves how to live, really live… to love the journey, not the destination.
—*Anna Quindlen*, A Short Guide to a Happy Life

A school counselor referred twelve-year-old Tim to me. Throughout the school year Tim had been easily agitated, resulting in bad behavior and detention. His mother Susan confirmed he'd always had a bad temper at home. I asked Tim's parents to accompany him to the first session. I asked the family my typical opening question as they arrived, so that I could understand their needs before asking The Miracle Question:

LM: What can we talk about today that would be helpful?

I received a quick response from Tim's father Gary:

GARY: Look, this is entirely my fault. I yell and curse at my family. Growing up, I came from a home where my dad abused me emotionally and verbally, so much so that I don't even remember half of my childhood. I think I have to change in order for Tim to change. I've worked on this for years and have gotten much better, but I still forget at times that the people in this room are my life. I'm not sure how I will help myself or Tim.

Can people who have grown up in miserable situations, where they are constantly put down and emotionally and verbally abused, change? Can they recover their dignity with their families after years of tormenting them as they were tormented? The answers will vary according to the professionals with whom you speak. My theory while working with The Miracle Question is that when people are given a chance to view themselves without their baggage, they are able to garner their expertise and make radical changes.

In this situation, Gary took the blame for his son's actions. If he'd continued to do this, there would be a good chance that Tim would continue to be angry and assume this was the legacy of his family. Instead, I took another approach in an effort to give the family an opportunity to change the pattern. I was impressed by Gary's integrity in admitting his faults and I told him so. He seemed a bit taken aback, as if he was expecting the same sort of verbal combat from me that he had received from his father when he was younger. Instead, I commended him on coming to counseling and admitting that he had a problem. Upon asking the family The Miracle Question, I received the following answers:

TIM: If a miracle happened, Mom wouldn't get so many calls from school. Instead, I would get better marks in citizenship and stay out of trouble. I would let stuff roll off my back and be less angry.

SUSAN: Everyone would get along at home. My son would control his anger at school and at home with his sisters. Gary would watch how he speaks to us.

GARY: Tim would do better in school with his temper and I would set a better example at home for all of them.

I asked Gary about his profession in an attempt to gather more exceptions, particularly since he was clearly a key to change. Whenever I inquire about a person's behavior in other situations, I can see him through a different lens. This technique ultimately provides me with information on my client's valuable competencies outside of the situation of concern.

Gary told me he was a foreman at a construction company. I asked if he ever supervised people. He said that he currently did. I asked him if he had ever lost his temper at work. He said that early in his career he had a tendency to let his temper fly but that his last boss had the same temperament as he did so he was never reprimanded.

However, his current boss did expect him to behave, and while he still lost his temper at times, it didn't happen as often.

I asked Gary about the times when his temper didn't control him, and he smiled. He said that luckily for him and his employees, his office was about five minutes away from where most of the employees worked so whenever someone did something he disliked, he had five minutes to settle down before they reported to him. By that time, he said, he was usually calmer and his temper wasn't as severe. These exceptions told me he had learned valuable strategies at work that he could not only use more often, but could also teach his son.

This information confirmed Gary could control his anger when he had some time before the confrontation *and* when he was expected to behave. This gave me an idea. I asked him about his expectations of Tim. He told me that he expected Tim to behave in school and at home with his sisters but, since he himself had a difficult time, he wondered how fair that was. I told him I wanted him to pretend that he was his son's supervisor for the next week. I also asked him to think of ways he had learned to control himself while taking a break from the session so I could talk to Tim privately.

Tim told me about the times in school when he did not get upset. There was one teacher, he said, who always complimented him and "stayed off everyone's back". He loved her class and did quite well in it. I asked him more about his home life and about the times when he did not let the anger habit take over at home. He told me about his two sisters who usually irritated him. On one occasion, his younger sister crept into his bedroom during a thunderstorm and lay on the end of his bed. He said it made him angry since she took up so much space. When I asked him if he became upset with her he said, "No, I just thought she was scared."

He also said at times he wanted more privacy but that he usually thought first about how his sisters looked up to him and that made him more patient with them. I was impressed. Like his father, Tim had the ability to control himself but he had failed to realize how he did so. Together, Tim and I wrote down the following strategies for him and his family to use for an experimental week, based only on the exceptions that Tim had shared with me.

Tim's personal strategies:

(a) Always think before saying anything.
(b) Realize that others are watching me.
(c) Think how others look up to me.
(d) Listen for compliments.

What Tim needs from his family:

(a) Tim responds better to people who compliment him often.
(b) Tim responds better when he knows others look up to him.

When the family reconvened, I asked Gary to help his son get control of the anger habit that bothered them both. I told him that I was impressed with the way he controlled his anger at work and felt strongly that his male influence over his son was indeed a valuable part of his son's new strategies. Gary said he had never thought of himself as "controlling himself" at work. He was simply glad that his employees were situated five minutes away. He said he'd never thought about how just taking some time had made a difference. He thought the problem bothered him all the time because he still reacted. He apparently forgot to notice times when he did not react as strongly. Those strategies and exceptions became his *Action Plan*. He told me he was ready to help Tim learn some strategies as he had. He had some ideas that just might do the trick.

I also asked Tim's parents to compliment Tim at times when they thought he would surely be upset but did not allow the habit to take over. I asked Tim to give them evidence that he was in control of the anger habit. He gladly accepted that challenge.

Susan returned with Tim in a week. She reported that not a single incident of anger had occurred in their home during the past week. She said Gary had surprised her on several occasions by his reactions to various situations when, formerly, he would have lost his temper. But, instead of yelling, he excused himself and took a break. She was both shocked and pleased. He then returned to talk to her calmly.

As for Tim, the reason they came to therapy in the first place? Well, he improved too. Tim did as his father did.

Changing Legacies by Changing Descriptions

What happened with Tim and Gary? In a forty-five minute session, a generational passing of the anger habit came to grips with the power of the human spirit and a legacy was changed for the better. This is not to say that both father and son might not someday face outbursts, but their success caused Tim and Gary's *system* to view them differently and decreased the likelihood that things would stay exactly the same. Gary's change of strategy toward Susan and the children would ultimately change their reaction to him, making him more approachable. Their attention may help him feel more patient and confident. This systemic change is contagious. It can change legacies and benefit future generations.

Therapist Michael White once implied that how people view themselves has a direct relationship to how they act. In other words, how we describe ourselves influences how we act and interact in our lives. Imagine then, that if the way you describe yourself keeps you stuck, perhaps it's time to *redescribe* yourself. For example, Gary told me that he was "emotionally and verbally abused". He said he was a childhood "victim" of his father. Since he viewed himself in that manner, he felt obliged to continue the legacy, thinking that since he still became angry, that there was nothing he could do about it. He had few options because of his perception. He failed to see times when he curtailed his anger with his employees as times when the anger could have taken him over.

When I told Gary I thought he had integrity and that I was impressed with the way that he'd expressed a need for help, he thought I was talking to someone else. My intention was to help him view himself differently. When I spoke to Tim about the anger habit, the problem became the issue, not him. Instead of being an angry person, he became a person bothered by an anger habit. Then he could formulate a strategy to control the habit. That's easier than changing yourself. As you begin to develop your Action Plan in this chapter, think of yourself as a person who has stepped out of a problem into a Miracle Day during which life works the way you want it to.

Exercise 4.1: Take Action with a New Image

The list of adjectives in the first column below includes typical descriptions from people who feel very stuck in their lives. The mere description often seems enough to trap a person from seeking solutions. In the second column, note what happens when the adjective is changed and defined differently.

Depressed	*Sad*
Sexually abused	*Has survived a tragic event*
Defiant	*Stands up for himself*
Hyperactive	*Energetic*
Argumentative	*Likes to express herself*

These are descriptions of the same feeling or circumstance that convey two very different messages. The first column is a typical list of diagnoses. While credible in themselves, the descriptions label the people, giving them cause to behave a certain way. For example, a sexual abuse *victim* will act very differently from a person who sees herself as a sexual abuse *survivor.* A different perception of a terrible incident makes all the difference. The victim may confine herself to platonic friendships, afraid that intimacy would be violent or invasive. The survivor will try to see the difference in each relationship and how partners can be different when compared to the perpetrator.

Each description labels a person in ways that can feel impossible to deal with. Not only does the second column present actions that we *can* deal with, it relieves us of thinking that we have to be experts to do so. For example, if we thought someone was depressed, we might feel immobilized to help him. But what if we thought of that same person as *sad*? We might be more likely to listen and try to help him. Someone who survived a tragic event might become someone we admired and looked to for help. The defiant person might become someone we could ask to help us when we needed support. The hyperactive person could become a person who was always ready to go and do (if we just help him focus on one task at a time!). We could always depend on the argumentative person to present a different side of the story.

Thinking of yourself and the people in your system in this way will allow your Action Plan to become more possible because you will momentarily suspend beliefs in order to perform. To begin, fill in the blanks below to start thinking of yourself differently:

Current descriptions of
myself and others:

New descriptions of
myself and others:

Myself:

_____   _____

_____   _____

Others:

_____   _____

_____   _____

_____   _____

_____   _____

Exercise 4.2: Action!

In an effort to measure your current actions in relation to what you want to achieve with your Action Plan, consider the following:

No miracle
occurring

Miracle is
achieved

| 1 | 2 | 3 | 4 | 5 | 6 | 7 | 8 | 9 | 10 |

On a scale of 1 to 10, with "10" indicating that you are achieving your miracle, write where you are now: _____

If your number is above "1" explain how you were able to achieve that (here comes another exception):

_____

_____

At what number on this scale would you like to be in a week? _____

Now let's review both the miracle goals you identified in Chapter Two and exceptions in Chapter Three so that we can get started on your Action Plan. Look at your goals from Chapter Two, your exceptions from Chapter Three and complete the following:

My Action Plan
I will begin doing the following for a day, or a week, based only on my exceptions:

1. _____

2. _____

3. _____

My Helpful Descriptions
How will I perceive myself and significant others in my life during this experimental time so that I will have the chance to be successful?

Myself:

_____

_____

Others:

_____

_____

Remember to Take Baby Steps, Bob!
Before you go to sleep tonight, plan how you will begin acting out a very small part of your miracle just for tomorrow given your plans or situation. Write your plan below:

_____

_____

_____

On the lines below, write what you hope someone will notice that you are doing differently, just for tomorrow:

_____

_____

_____

Conclusion

Your Action Plan is your homework assignment. Guarantee yourself that it will be successful by making sure that the strategies you wrote in the worksheets in this chapter are from exceptions only. They are proof that you know what to do. Pair them with helpful descriptions, and take things slowly, making sure you're prepared for what your system needs from you.

The plan you have just composed is the first step towards obtaining your miracle. Your life has now begun to change just by answering the few questions in this book. You will now look at today and tomorrow differently because you will think of yourself differently. Even better, the people in your life are about to be "re-introduced" to a person of hope. Give them something to see.

> Things do not change; we change.
> —*Henry David Thoreau*

Chapter Five

Recognize Your Success

Know what's weird? Day by day, nothing seems to change,
but pretty soon… everything's different.
—*Calvin from Calvin and Hobbes*

Pick up any tabloid and you'll read about famous people who have revealed their tragic childhoods, substance abuse problems, sexual abuse problems, eating disorders and marital discord. Awful secrets and terrible circumstances bear descriptions that appall us. These revered celebrities have truly had their share of challenges. People read about these celebrities and feel sorry for them. It seems unfair that *anyone* should experience the trials and tribulations that life has brought them.

But look who they have become in spite of their difficulties! That alone should be celebrated, not their tribulations and dark secrets. They rose above their shame and despair, unhappiness and stressful situations, poverty and lack of education to excel in their fields and become people others admire, even idolize. They should be recognized for their triumph over those trials. They're proof that people can be resilient.

What Does Your Personal Tabloid Say About You?

In Chapter One, you brainstormed your miracle and in Chapter Two, you evaluated it. In Chapter Three you discovered some exceptions and used them to design your Action Plan in Chapter Four. Things are somehow different for you, even if you or the significant others in your life haven't noticed those differences yet. As the quote at the beginning of this chapter states, "Day by day, nothing seems to change". But if you continue to follow your miracle, pretty soon things will be radically different.

Recognizing what *has* gone better can be difficult for those of us who are steeped in the problems that force us into despair. It's easier to describe what goes wrong in our day rather than what went right. Those situations get in our way and curb our routine. But to notice what works will bring your Miracle to life. If you believe nothing has changed for you, perhaps the next few scenarios will help you to realize that change really can and does happen, and that it is already happening to you.

Taking the Risk to Live Again

Debbie's boyfriend Jim was killed in a car accident on the way to her house. A diamond ring was found in the wreckage—he had apparently planned to propose to her that night. Tormented by many months of depression and anxiety, she came to counseling through the urging of her boss. A professional woman with years of success in a governmental agency, she had isolated herself from friends, family and workers for months. She rarely left the house except to go to work. Her family were worried about her lack of motivation to socialise and her boss was considering asking for her resignation. When she came to counseling, it was clear she recognized the need to begin getting her life back together again. I asked The Miracle Question. She responded:

DEBBIE: In a miracle, I would be willing to take a risk. That's what it's going to take to get back into life. Something will have to jolt me into it. I have to do this on my own. I have always been good at doing things to get ahead, but this thing, this event has set me back so much.

LM: Tell me about times before Jim's death, when you were into life, and were enjoying things more.

DEBBIE: When he and I went to Hawaii we went parasailing. I had an absolute blast. Here I was, a starched professional type, high above the ocean. It was terrific. I used to love taking risks like that… I can't believe I just told you that. I'd forgotten about doing things like that until now. Wow. I have really been hiding.

LM: Sounds to me like you have taken risks before. Tell me about other times when you took risks at work or with friends.

Debbie told me about the risks she took at work that had gained her credibility. She told me about her many friends and recalled other times when, together, they had taken risks. Before the session was over, I asked her to do only one thing during the next week, on a small scale, that would be considered slightly risky. She agreed.

She returned a week later dressed differently. During her first session she had come in a business suit. For this session she arrived in jeans and a T-shirt. She was going out after the session, she said with a smile. But the best was yet to come:

DEBBIE: I hope I didn't go overboard, but after I left last week, all the way home I thought about risk-taking and realized that, originally, that was who I was. I let my guard down a little and got invited to a party. The party was something else... I ended up going skinny-dipping in a hot tub. I guess I took a risk!

Debbie got an "A" on her homework assignment.

The Enabler Gets a Gift

When I began to work as a school counselor, several colleagues warned me to not give a certain student's mother too much of my time. I was told that Beth liked to call her son Ken's teachers and counselor each week and lament his poor grades and his Attention Deficit Disorder. I was told I shouldn't enable her to keep enabling him. Being of a different mindset, I perceived Beth as passionate the first time she called, and felt she'd probably been through a lot with Ken. I actually looked forward to her calls after that. She not only called me often, I called her too. In fact, I found that when I gave her what she wanted—my time and support—she called me less. Things went rather well until the last month of Ken's senior year. One morning Beth called me frantically:

BETH: I want Ken's school work modified today! I've watched him struggle for thirteen years. I was at the grocery store yesterday and overheard a parent talking about the radical difference that having a modified curriculum made for his thirteen-year-old son. Why hasn't someone told me about this all these years? I feel Ken has been cheated. It would have made a world of difference for all of us.

It was mid-April of his senior year. He would graduate the next month. I knew from looking at his grades that he would never have qualified for a modified plan because his IQ and achievement tests were average. I could have told Beth it was too late to change his curriculum. I could even have said, "I'll check into the possibility of a modification" or told her that doing so would be impossible. Instead, I chose another route.

LM: Let's think about this a moment. I think it's most remarkable that, yes, a modified plan might have made things better for Ken, but in spite of his not being modified, he has succeeded in passing his classes. Granted, he didn't make all A's, but he passed. Do you know what that means about your son? It means that in spite of his challenges, he made it. You must be so proud.

BETH: I suppose I am proud. He has struggled. He has ADD and school has always been tough for him. He has always needed extra attention from us at home and tutors to make it.

DM: And in spite of ADD and the struggle, in four weeks your son will graduate from high school. He has learned that when he struggles, getting the additional help from you and tutoring ensures that he can make it. You have actually given him a gift.

Our conversation gradually ended without any other requests. Her son graduated the following month. He enrolled at a college several states away and made it through his freshman year with typical, but far from overwhelming, struggles.

"It's Always Awful... Well, Maybe Not Always"

Remember what I said earlier about "always"? Early in my career as a family therapist, I worked at an adolescent treatment center where kids in trouble with the law or disruptive at home lived for several months at a time. I recall Jerry, a fifteen-year-old who was placed at the center by his single mother, Carol, after he ran away and was violent towards her at home. Jerry did quite well after a few weeks of learning the rules and consequences of his actions. He was soon a popular patient who became quite helpful to others on the unit. Our discharge meeting went well. Carol was given various techniques to use with Jerry if he relapsed. She had also been enrolled in some parent meetings to learn better parenting skills. She and Jerry left with a wealth of information to help them succeed.

At our first follow-up meeting I was surprised to hear Carol say "things were just terrible again… he will never change". I was perplexed. How could an adolescent who had done so well at our facility have relapsed in only two weeks? I knew there must have been some good times during that time period.

LM: I know you're saying things aren't working well right now, but I'm interested in how many days over the past two weeks things went okay.

JERRY: Until yesterday, she and I got along great.

CAROL: Yesterday was awful. He was screaming at me and I was on his tail. I figured it was all going to start over again.

LM: Carol, do you agree that until yesterday everything was alright?

CAROL: I suppose things were definitely better until yesterday.

LM: Jerry, you were discharged two weeks ago. How many of the fourteen days would you say went better than before you came to this facility?

JERRY: I guess thirteen.

CAROL: I think he's right.

LM: You know, Carol, that's quite a success rate, thirteen out of fourteen days. What was Jerry doing during those thirteen days that worked? Jerry, what did your mom do that worked?

Jerry and Carol left the session realizing that there would be some pitfalls, but for the most part, it was more helpful to identify the days that went better than talk about the problem. Their assignment was to keep a calendar showing the days that worked and the days that didn't. Because they were committed to watching each other so closely for what worked, they began showing more respect toward each other and noting what they appreciated about each other. They settled into telling me what did work in our future sessions.

Common Threads Weave Similar Miracles

What does each of these scenarios have in common? They each involved people seeing only problems and not exceptions, until they learned to recognize their exceptions. Stuck in stories that only seemed to be headed for unhappy endings, they seemed unaware of their abilities at first and were ready to settle into a pattern of blaming. They were too focused on pinpointing their problems to take a break, step back and look at the times when the problems did not intrude. When they did, solutions emerged. How did they do it?

- They began perceiving themselves as successful by taking note of successful actions and situations. That gave them confidence to do more of the same.

- They learned to feel more secure in their planning because they recognized that using their previous strategies was a no-fail opportunity. They couldn't lose.

- They began to complain less about situations because they were given assignments to watch for the opposite of adversity… times when life worked better. Doing this made them act differently in their system, and the system changed as a result.

Exercise 5.1: The Daily Mental Check—What's Better?

What went better today, yesterday or any day at work, home, with the kids, with friends, physically, emotionally, socially since you started your Action Plan?

_____

_____

_____

_____

_____

How did you perceive yourself as you began making these changes?

As a person who:

_____

_____

_____

_____

What thoughts kept you on track as you began making the changes?

I thought about:

_____

_____

_____

_____

On a scale of 1 to 10, with 10 meaning that you've completely accomplished your miracle, where are you today?

_____

On the same scale, where would you like to be in a week?

_____

How will you do that?

I will think about:

_____

_____

_____

I will perceive myself as a person who:

_____

_____

_____

I know I am this person because:

_____

_____

As a result, I will do the following action for the next day/few days/ week:

_____

_____

_____

Exercise 5.2: Some Miracles Need a "Plan B"

Life happens. Things might not have gone as well as you had planned initially, but don't give up. Instead, write what you forgot to do, think about, or anything else that got in the way over the past few days:

What thoughts and situations got in the way of pursuing your miracle for the past few days?

_____

_____

What actions seemed difficult to achieve recently?

_____

_____

_____

How can you break down the actions into smaller ones or think slightly differently for a day or two so that you can slowly begin to work on your Action Plan?

_____

_____

_____

What do you need to do regarding your system so that you are more likely to try new strategies for a day or two?

_____

_____

_____

Conclusion

Situations intrude on our plans at times. It's normal for clients who first struggle with difficult issues to come back later having made just a few changes. Things rarely go perfectly. Life just isn't like that. We don't all have cheerleaders on the sidelines. Some of us have to make the goal all on our own. Consider the following passage from *The Millionaire Mind* by Thomas P. Stanley:

> You recently completed undergraduate school and now you are contemplating pursuing a graduate degree. Before you are admitted, you must take the Graduate Record Exam (GRE). Several weeks after you take the exam, your scores arrive in the mail … Your quantitative score places you in the bottom 10 percent and you are in the bottom quarter for tests in physics, chemistry, biology, social studies and the fine arts. How many counselors would be likely to say to you:

> "Young man, you have extraordinary leadership qualities, great vision. Some day you will change the social conscience of America. You will have more to do with social and political changes in America than anyone since FDR."

Probably few counselors would have said that to a young Martin Luther King, Jr. Certainly, if they had recognized his strengths, perseverance and courage, they would have looked past his deficits and focused on what he did well. He recognized what he had to do. Luckily for the world he took his scores in stride and became the legend he was in spite of them.

As you continue with your Action Plan, recognize the times in your morning, afternoon and evening when conversations work better and are more enjoyable. Watch how and when chores get done more smoothly. Realize when a good mood emerges and laughter happens. Notice when your anger disappears and yesterday's anxiety seems miles away. Jot down all of these discoveries in the pages of the last chapter as a journal. These are the times when the strategies you are trying to perform are already happening. Notice and be proud. Recognize yourself.

Happiness is a butterfly, which when pursued, is always just beyond
your grasp, but which if you sit down quietly, may alight upon you.
—*Nathaniel Hawthorne*

Chapter Six

Give Your Marriage a Miracle

> At the touch of love everyone becomes a poet.
> —*Plato*

Once upon a time, two people met. They discovered they had mutual interests and enjoyed many of the same activities. They became attracted to each other. They felt satisfied and understood, so they fell in love, decided to commit to each other, and promised to live happily ever after, no matter what.

Most of the time, inevitably, the "no matter what" happens. The marriage is challenged by trials, tribulations, old or new expectations, additions and temptations that step in its path. The couple either absorbs the interfering situations with good faith and adapts to them or dissolves the relationship because of them. When they are ready to dissolve the marriage, they sometimes spend a lot of time and money analyzing what went wrong. Sometimes insight saves the marriage but more often than not, it simply provides information.

This chapter is about saving marriages by focusing on the strengths couples sometimes forget they had when their relationship was new and their marriage working. It's about identifying and discovering methods couples used previously to absorb life's interferences and survive its storms. It's about resiliency and focuses on rewriting your love story when the world has threatened to change the characters in your fairy tale.

Before Going Forward, Go Backward

In their book, *Love is a Verb,* Pat Hudson and Bill O'Hanlon describe what happens to people when marriage goes awry:

When things go wrong in our relationships, we are all inclined to look at our mates and conclude that they have got the personality problem, and if only they would fix the problem, everything would be better. If it's not a personality problem, perhaps it's a life event. "He's never worked through his father's death and he takes it out on me." Or, "She has a conflict with her boss, but I get the flack." The difficulty with this line of thinking is that we will continue to see our mates as the cause of the pattern and nothing will change.

In Chapter One, Felix and Elaine were on the verge of divorce. Below are the answers the couple gave to The Miracle Question as we began working together:

ELAINE: In our miracle we would be best friends again. We would be doing things that we did then—dancing, hiking, talking, talking and more talking."

FELIX: The kids would be better behaved and we would share the responsibility for them.

ELAINE: We would sit down and plan together for a change, like we used to.

FELIX: In the miracle, she would look up from her book when I came home and be glad to see me.

Felix and Elaine thought they needed to reinvent their marriage. They thought they needed new ideas to do so. In the dialog above, they talked about what they used to do that worked. These are the *exceptions* that compose their miracle. Naturally, having children will change a couple's roles. There are additional responsibilities, exhausting chores, activities and challenges. Looking further back into Felix and Elaine's life pre-children, I learned that they shared responsibility equally for their pets, finances, home upkeep and more. I asked how they did that and they said they discussed what needed to be done and decided how they would do it together.

Initially, many couples handle chores in this way and when children come along or job responsibilities change, they no longer sit down and decide how to do things together. The same goes for the dancing, hiking and talking Felix and Elaine used to do. Those activities may have looked different with the addition of three children, but the activities themselves still brought enjoyment to the couple. How they would adapt their current life to those and other fun activities would be a challenge.

As for the dilemma Felix felt regarding his attraction to Elaine, it was helpful for Elaine to tell him what she liked him doing when they were first married. Sure, sometimes lust and love just took over, but he was more thoughtful during those days and she was less tired after work. He told her he felt attractive when she met him at the door with a smile and they would save the problems of the day for later. Together, they both tried to look at what worked before.

Felix vs. Elaine: Moving Toward the Goal

All of this may mean that the way Elaine behaved had something to do with Felix's reaction to her and vice versa. With this in mind, I wanted to help the couple talk about other times when each felt important to the other. I presented a different kind of scale.

I drew the scale on a large white board and wrote each goal below the number "5".

Felix				Goals				Elaine
1	2	3	4	5	4	3	2	1

Planning for family needs or activities together.
Feeling more attracted to each other and giving each other attention.
Going hiking, dancing or doing other activities they used to do.
Talking more.

Then we had the following conversation that helped us to discuss the items listed under "goals":

LM: You're both quite lucky. You both agree on these goals. Let's talk about where each of you is on this scale. Where would you place yourself in relation to doing whatever it takes to accomplish these goals?

FELIX: I think I would be at a 2 because I really haven't tried lately.

ELAINE: I think I do more than he does, so probably a 3.

LM: Felix, where would you put Elaine on the scale in relation to what she has tried to make things work for both of you and accomplish these goals?

FELIX: I think she does try harder than I do so probably a 3½.

LM: Elaine, where would you put Felix on the scale in relation to what he has tried to do so that things work for both of you and accomplish these goals?

ELAINE: I think about a 2½, because lately he has been more attentive to me.

LM: Think back to a better time when these goals were happening a bit more. Who did what to make them happen?

FELIX: I had a different job so I helped with the kids more.

ELAINE: We went out occasionally and my mother, who has now moved away, kept the children and I didn't worry about them.

LM: What else?

FELIX: I weighed less. I used to work out.

ELAINE: We both set time to talk more and I knew more about his life. Now I don't feel I know him very well.

LM: From what you have just described to me, what would you suggest doing so that you move up the scale towards the goals just for the next week?

FELIX: I think we need to go hiking and take the kids. They have never been hiking and it would give us all a break from the usual dull weekend.

ELAINE: Maybe we should sit down together and plan the hiking without the kids interrupting us, maybe after they are in bed. We can plan like we used to, where we would go, where we would camp and what we need to take with us. That was fun then.

While I was a little cautious about the couple taking the kids with them on their trip, I was also intrigued by their willingness to work on a plan as they had in the past. They left with a strategy and both knew that they needed to participate in that strategy. They are still together and their children are enjoying fairly frequent hiking and camping trips. They have a new babysitter and get some videos for the kids to watch when Felix comes home in the evening to give them time to talk to each other. Felix is looking for a job that will allow him to come home earlier in the evening.

Exercise 6.1: Scaling Your Marriage from the Outside In

The following exercise can be enlightening if your marriage is off track. It is helpful to do the exercise together but if you find that only you are at the point of working on the marriage, you can still benefit from the answers.

1.   Answer The Miracle Question:

Suppose tonight while you sleep, a miracle happens. When you awake tomorrow morning, how will your marriage to each other be different?

Spouse 1

_____

_____

_____

Spouse 2

_____

_____

_____

When this miracle begins to happen in your marriage, what will the answers you just gave do for each of you?

Spouse 1

_____

_____

_____

Spouse 2

_____

_____

_____

Find the exceptions. Take a trip back to a time when your marriage worked well.

Describe the times when some of the goals above occurred. What was different and who did what?

Spouse 1

_____

_____

_____

Spouse 2

_____

_____

_____

When your lives were interrupted, how did you manage the situation in a way you were proud of?

Spouse 1

_____

_____

_____

Spouse 2

_____

_____

_____

What did your spouse do for you during the good times that endeared him/her to you?

Spouse 1

_____

_____

_____

Spouse 2

_____

2. Scale your relationship:

On the scale below, write the goals from task 1 that you both agree would help your marriage to get back on track. Write them below number 5 on the lines provided:

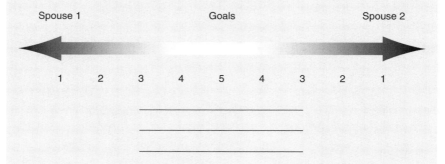

Spouse 1   Goals   Spouse 2

1   2   3   4   5   4   3   2   1

_____
_____
_____

Taking turns, rate yourself on how hard you have tried to achieve the above goals below:

Spouse 1 _____

Spouse 2 _____

Taking turns, rate each other on how hard you think your spouse has tried to achieve the goals above:

Spouse 1 rates Spouse 2 at _____

Spouse 2 rates Spouse 1 at _____

3. Design your Action Plan:

Based on the information you described in task 2, tell your spouse what he/she could begin doing just for a week (or a day) that would help him/her move up slightly on the scale:

Spouse 1 to Spouse 2:

_____

_____

_____

_____

Spouse 2 to Spouse 1:

_____

_____

_____

_____

4.   Designate a time to review your success each day:

_____

When You Need to Make Amends

In their book, *Rewriting Love Stories,* Hudson and O'Hanlon mention the importance of making amends when one partner has violated personal or physical boundaries:

> The first (step) is to acknowledge his actions in the matter without making excuses. This is the accountability piece. He does not have to accept blame, just responsibility. The second repairing move is for the violator to offer to make amends in some way or to restore trust … one man offered to let his wife call him or drop in on him at any time when he was at work or any social event to reassure her that he was no longer lying to her about where he was … one woman wrote her partner an apology for having hit her and promised never to get physically violent again in the relationship.

What if You Could Rewrite the Fairy Tale?

Couples that endure hardship in their relationships may want to try to make the marriage or relationship work, but feelings sometimes persevere, and unless the couple can begin to leave negative thoughts or words about the past behind, the chances of working things out will lessen.

David Epson and Michael White have acknowledged the art of storytelling in therapy in their book, *Narrative Means to Therapeutic Ends*. As you read through the next paragraph, think about how your lives together compose a story, ever changing and evolving, with plots and climaxes that don't always prepare you for what is happening:

> Our lives are ceaselessly intertwined with narrative, with the stories we tell and hear told, those we dream or imagine or would like to tell, all of which are reworked in the story of our own lives that we narrate to ourselves in an episodic, sometimes semi-conscious, but virtually uninterrupted monologue.

Within this intricate message, consider this: Your marriage is a story. Whatever point you are at, consider it one or two chapters in a story that you promised each other would last a lifetime. Sometimes characters are written into the story that interrupt or enhance our story. Other times characters that were vital to our story leave us and we feel alone.

The next exercise is rather simple—it's an opportunity to rewrite your fairy tale. A variation of The Miracle Question, it is another way to begin writing the story you wish to create for yourself and your spouse. Maybe there will be characters you would like to omit. Maybe there will be activities that need to be altered. Perhaps the excitement needs to be increased and the stress decreased. However your revision looks, write it as you want it to be.

Then, realize that you have the power to rewrite your story each day. Choose to make the day a paragraph in your chapter that you wish to read and read again. Delete the paragraphs of days that don't work. Stay on track with your new chapter by knowing where you are going (the answer to The Miracle Question) and watching closely just how you get there.

Exercise 6.2: Our New Fairy Tale

Below, write the memorable and not so memorable characters, actions, situations and experiences your marriage has encountered in your Chapter One.

Memorable:

_____

_____

_____

_____

_____

_____

_____

_____

Not so Memorable:

_____

_____

_____

_____

_____

_____

_____

_____

_____

_____

_____

As you write Chapter Two together, describe the influential characters, situations or beliefs you would like to change:

Characters:

_____

_____

_____

_____

Situations:

_____

_____

_____

_____

Beliefs:

_____

_____

_____

_____

_____

Write how you want your Chapter Two to begin:

_____

_____

_____

_____

When you look back over Chapter Two fifty years from now, what do hope to see?

_____

_____

_____

_____

The time in between will lead you from one point to another. Use your strengths and abilities as a couple and as individuals to get there together.

Conclusion

This poem was read at my son, Roger Jr.'s college graduation. While it begins with a funeral, it ends with another very valuable question.

The Dash
By Linda Ellis

I read of a man, who stood to speak, at the funeral of a friend.
He referred to the dates to be put on her tombstone, from the beginning
—to the end.

He noted that first came the date of her birth,
And spoke of the following date with tears,
But he said what mattered most of all, was the DASH between those years.

For that DASH represents all the time that she spent alive on earth,
And now only those who loved her know what that little line is worth.

For it matters not how much we won;
The cars… the house… the cash.
What matters is how we live and love, and how we spend our "DASH".

So think about this long and hard…
Are there things you'd like to change?
For you never know how much time is left.
(You could be at "DASH mid-range".)

If we could just slow down enough to consider what's true and real,
And love the people in our lives, like we've never loved before.

If we treat each other with respect and more often wear a smile…
Remembering that our special DASH might only last awhile.

So, when your eulogy is being read, with your life's actions to rehash…
Would you be proud of the things they say, about how you spent your DASH.

Chapter Seven
Parenting Your Small Miracle

If you have built castles in the air, your work need not be lost. That is
where they should be. Now put the foundation under them.
—*Henry David Thoreau*

Every therapist has a memorable case that challenges and makes
us smile. Josh was mine. Six years old, blond and blue-eyed, full of
energy and feistiness, he greeted *me* with his parents Michelle and
Ben and little brother Sam the first time his family came for
counseling:

JOSH: Hi, Dr. Metcalf, my name is Josh. I'm here with my mother,
father and brother, Sam. My parents told me we were coming to
see you because I can't be the boss in the family anymore. I like
being the boss. You have to tell them I am the boss.

He really did say that.

Josh and I walked down the hallway to my office, parents following behind with Sam. Once inside, he was into everything, including my filing cabinet, handbag and toy box. He seemed to have no
boundaries whatsoever. His parents seemed frustrated and anxious that he might damage something. I began to get anxious
myself. Michelle began:

MICHELLE: This is why we're here. Josh has been expelled from
three first grade classes. He is now on probation at his school,
where he sits in a classroom alone. We have been to four other
therapists, so you are our last hope. We have tried all sorts of
discipline strategies and none of them work. He won't sit in
time-out. He doesn't care if his toys are placed in a garbage bag
and then put on the curb for the garbage truck. He hits his
brother, fights with the kids at school because he wants to be in
charge. We're at our wits' end.

I asked Josh to take a break and visit my secretary, Tami. I began The Miracle Question process with the parents because it was clear that this family really needed it.

MICHELLE: In our miracle, we would have a peaceful family life where Josh listened to us and knew we were in charge. He would behave in school, respect his teachers and know that he is a child, not an adult.

LM: Tell me about times when he behaves slightly better and sees you as being in charge.

MICHELLE: Those times are rare. I am a stay-at-home mom and taking care of Sam is a handful. It's hard to keep things on track.

BEN: Yeah, she tries but he just won't listen.

The parents had tried all sorts of interventions and read many books about discipline to no avail. I turned to Ben:

LM: Tell me what you do for a living.

BEN: I'm in sales. I travel a lot and I know that doesn't help her much. I have reps to check on constantly and make sure that they do their jobs, so even when I'm home, I'm preoccupied.

LM: Do you supervise people, like other salespeople?

BEN: Yes, I've supervised other salespeople for over seven years.

LM: Have you ever had employees who didn't recognize you as being in charge?

BEN: (*laughing*) Boy, does that happen.

LM: What do you do to help them realize that you are in charge?

BEN: I send lots of reminders to them with memos about expectations of their performance. I've followed some of them around to make sure they are doing what they're supposed to. I'm actually up for a promotion soon.

LM: I have an idea, based on what you've just told me. I would like you to think of Josh as a supervisee for the next two weeks. Use whatever skills you already use at work with him, to let him know that you and your wife are in charge. Know what I mean?

Ben sat right up and nodded. Michelle grinned widely.

Two weeks later they arrived again and things seemed different. Ben and Josh came in hand-in-hand. The family, Michelle and Sam first, then Ben and Josh, walked down the hall in front of me. Upon entering the room, Josh asked Ben if he could play with the checkers on top of the toy box. Ben told him he could. Josh played quietly next to his little brother. Michelle looked as if she would burst with excitement.

MICHELLE: I can't recall the last time we have had such a peaceful week. The first week was a bit hairy but this past week has been unbelievable.

LM: What have you done as a family that has made such a difference?

BEN: I arranged to stay home for the first week to help out. I decided to supervise Mr. Josh and let him know who was boss. It was tough, believe me. I had no idea what Michelle went through each day. What I did, though, was follow him around. When he needed to go to time-out, I sat with him and held him in his chair. He got upset at first, but later, he got the idea. When he needed to clean up after himself and wouldn't, I sat on the floor of his room with the door closed and informed him that I wasn't leaving until he finished what he needed to do.

All this time, Josh was listening attentively while playing with Sam. I could see him out of the corner of my eye, glancing at his dad as he talked. Suddenly, he couldn't contain himself any longer, and jumped up.

JOSH: Dad's right, Dr. Metcalf. He told me if I didn't straighten up and behave, he was going to 'write me up'. Then, I was gonna get fired! I'm not the boss of the family anymore, exactly. Mom and Dad are the bosses and I am the assistant boss of Sam. I'm bigger than he is so I can tell him what to do sometimes, when Dad says it's okay.

Ben couldn't have been prouder as we all roared with laughter. Josh just smiled and sat down proudly next to his brother, enjoying the attention. Several years later, a follow-up revealed that Josh had been admitted into the gifted and talented program at his elementary school, was in Boy Scouts, and played soccer and baseball. He was a leader in each of these activities, always volunteered to do more than his share, but he learned to ask first. Both parents continued to maintain a "supervisory" program with Josh and both agreed that Josh would probably grow up to be President. (This case is taken in part from my book *Parenting Toward Solutions*.)

What?! Take My Work Home With Me?

In the same way that The Miracle Question assumes people can develop ideas and strategies from what they've done successfully in the past, when parenting skills are at issue they can learn to tap into their expertise from other areas. Ben's skills as a supervisor transitioned as parenting skills for an energetic and challenging little boy. It was distressing that his parents had tried other methods without success. Because experts developed those methods, when Ben failed to respond, they felt something was wrong with him.

Using a solution-focused approach through The Miracle Question, when Dad realized that he had the skills, his confidence improved and he followed through. In this chapter, The Miracle Question will take you through another stage and provide you with ideas for parenting your children.

Just What the Doctor Ordered

Many "miracle days" involve changing the way children, particularly adolescents, respond to their parents. Parents sometimes think therapists should somehow adjust the teenager's attitude or simply tell them how to change their adolescent's behavior. I've never met anyone who's successfully changed another person against his or her will, especially an adolescent, but I have met and worked with many parents who, by changing *their* actions, brought about huge changes in their children's.

Jeremy was just such a father who was able to cause a change in his rebellious fifteen-year-old daughter Leslie. He'd tried grounding, yelling and threatening. In return he was treated to Leslie's "attitude" and more misbehavior. I listened to his complaints and then asked him The Miracle Question, and we worked through the rest of the process together.

JEREMY: In my miracle day my daughter would respect me. She would talk to me and listen to me.

LM: What would that do for you?

JEREMY: It would mean that she respected me.

LM: Tell me about other people who respect you.

JEREMY: I'm a physician in charge of an entire maternity ward. My staff knows I'm going to be there no matter what. They don't question me. I've been there for ten years. They respect me.

LM: What would they say you do that earns their respect?

JEREMY: I'm dependable. I respect them and they respect me. I'm patient with them. I talk to them and try to be understanding of their needs, and I compliment them when they go out of their way to help a patient or me. I also tow the line. They know what they are expected to do. We are a real team.

LM: Do you ever get upset at work?

JEREMY: Sure, doesn't everybody?

LM: When you react to something that makes you angry, how do you maintain your staff's respect?

JEREMY: I stay calm. I stay professional. I may walk off for a minute and tell the staff member I'll be back to talk in a while. In a hospital, patients don't need to see you upset. I give the staff member time to talk but I don't back down from what needs to happen.

LM: Those are great strategies. How are they different from those you use when you're upset with Leslie?

JEREMY: They're very different.

LM: I wonder what might happen over the next week if your daughter gets upset and you use the same strategy that you use at work with her.

JEREMY: *(laughing)* She would probably wonder what was wrong with me.

LM: I'd like to give you an assignment based on what works so well with your staff. As you leave here today, I'd like you to visualize creating the same sort of relationship with your daughter you have with the people at work. You said you support and listen to your staff's ideas, that you compliment them when they do things well and that, when you have to correct them, you walk away, gather your thoughts, and then talk to them calmly. Is this all correct?

JEREMY: Yes.

LM: Then it sounds like you know what to do, based on what you've told me works in the hospital. I'll look forward to learning how you carry this out with Leslie. Make sure you watch for her reactions.

Two weeks later, Jeremy reported he'd only been treated to Leslie's attitude once. He'd asked her to run errands with him on a few occasions and she went without complaint. He also asked to go with her to the mall, which surprised her. He expected her to refuse but instead, she surprised him both with her willingness and the fun they had. He enjoyed their time together and told her she was fun to be with. When she got upset at not having permission to attend a party, instead of yelling, Jeremy explained why he said no—he didn't know the friend's parents, so she wasn't allowed to go. He also told her that he was doing this because he loved her. She calmed down slightly and told him she'd bring the friend over sometime in the future. He said he looked forward to meeting the friend. Leslie still wasn't happy with Jeremy's decision, but the conversation changed from a confrontation to a calm discussion.

Exercise 7.1: The Personal Survey of Professional and Personal Skills

Your personal and professional skills can assist you in parenting, too. By doing the following survey, you will see just how much they can help.

A. List the qualities, habits, and skills required to perform your job efficiently (examples: punctuality, organization, interpersonal skills, intelligence etc.). Next to each quality, note briefly how you manage to demonstrate this quality (what you are thinking about, doing, showing others etc.):

1. _____

2. _____

3. _____

4. _____

5. _____

B. How would your boss describe your most valuable qualities and skills:

1. _____

2. _____

3. _____

4. _____

5. _____

C. Explain the qualities and skills you use when working with co-workers or good friends that contribute to your good relationships. Briefly note how you manage to show these qualities (what do you think about, believe, say etc.?):

1. _____

2. _____

3. _____

4. _____

5. _____

D. Ask your spouse or partner how he/she would describe your *behavior* when the "good times" occur with your children:

1. _____

2. _____

3. _____

4. _____

5. _____

E. Imagine using a video camera and capturing a better relationship with your children on tape. What do you see yourself doing that would tell you the relationships were better?

_____

_____

_____

_____

F. If you interviewed your children, how would they describe the *ideal* relationship with you?

_____

_____

_____

_____

Walk This Way, Talk This Way

Sometimes stepping into the shoes of your children can give you a completely different perspective on their world. Twelve-year-old Andy came with his parents to a counseling session. I asked him what I would experience if I walked around in his shoes all day. He replied with a smirk:

ANDY: You wouldn't last until noon. You would be woken by your mom who worked at the same school you went to and had to be there earlier than you did every day. Then you would hang around and wait as she talked to all your teachers every day about whether you were being good or not. Then, when you came home, you would get no break … just homework, homework, homework. And, to make it worse, when Dad came home, he would want to spend time with you watching a hockey game on TV but Mom would come in and argue with him that you needed to be in bed. It never gets better. That's why I get so stressed out and lose my temper all the time.

Andy's parents had no idea that they were being obstinate with each other—and with him. After he shared these comments, we began talking about what could make his day less stressful, keeping the expectations of behaving in school and doing his schoolwork. Both parents agreed to a schedule that would accommodate Andy's need to spend time with his dad and respect his need to be a regular student at school instead of a teacher's son. Within days, Andy's temper was tamed and his attitude became calmer.

So, Johnny, What Do You Think About the War?

Children, particularly adolescents, have their own perspectives, and we should pay attention to and respect them by listening to their thoughts and opinions on whatever is important to them. With the unfortunate global conflicts that have emerged over the past few years, talking to your children has never been more crucial. A current television commercial depicts parents and kids talking about daily experiences while eating, driving and doing chores. When you talk to your children about everyday events, tackling subjects like smoking and drug use becomes easier, even natural.

Talking to your children about your job, the news and what's going on in their lives not only helps you know them, it better prepares you for the trials that typically come during their later years. Try fostering that better relationship by using the following technique the next time you get upset. Ask yourself the following question before exploding:

"What goal do I want to achieve with my son or daughter right now?"

Get her attention.
Show him a better way to do something.

Keep her safe.

Help him discover a better way to solve a problem.

The manner in which you approach your goal will make all the difference to how your child or adolescent listens to you. During a child development course I taught to college sophomores, the topic of discipline was raised. As we went through the various types of disciplinary actions parents use, I asked them what their parents had done when they were younger that had made a lasting impression on them. It wasn't grounding or punishing them that worked. Instead, most said that when they were told their parents were *disappointed* in their behavior that was the worst punishment they could have been given.

Talk to your children—particularly your adolescents. Give them parents to respect. Your actions speak louder than words and what you think about them matters. Watch your words. Children learn what they see. They remember what you do with them. Walk in their shoes for a day.

Parenting Adolescents: Actions vs. Reactions

The previous section talked about building a better relationship with your child. A colleague, Stephen Chilton, facilitates a solution-focused parenting group for the parents of adolescents. Chilton discusses several assumptions with parents during the first session in an effort to help them perceive their role differently. Notice the simplicity and respectful quality of each assumption:

- Parenting is the most difficult job that you will ever love.
- You deserve the same love and respect that you give to your son/daughter.
- Parenting is a continuous call to learn about the best and worst in yourselves.
- Remember, as a parent, "… the love you take is equal to the love you make…"

As The Miracle Question process has conveyed, when parents respond differently to a problem, there will ultimately be a new result. One way to begin formulating new responses is to think of your adolescent *differently*.

Exercise 7.2: The Redescription Prescription

I use this activity with parenting groups to change the participants' perspectives about kids:

1. Describe your adolescent's attitude or actions during the times when you are most concerned. Write your answers under "Descriptions" below.

2. When you describe your adolescent that way, how do you react to him/her? Write your answers under "Reactions".

Descriptions   Reactions
Defiant   *I get defensive*

_____   _____

_____   _____

_____   _____

_____   _____

3. Let's keep the original description you wrote, only this time, pre-tend you're describing a best friend or dear relative. Let's say you've known this person all your life and she is very important to you. You've shared secrets, challenges and frustrations. Suppose you suddenly see your friend the way you have listed above under "Descriptions". Below, list those same descriptions. How might you react differently? Write those answers under New Reactions:

Descriptions   New Reactions

_____   _____

_____   _____

_____   _____

_____   _____

Were the reactions you listed to question 3 different from those in question 2? This exercise illustrates an important point: That you value your children as much if not more than significant others in your life. Through this exercise you've developed some new ways to respond the next time your adolescent acts out.

4. Using the descriptions and new reactions from question 3, imagine you began to react to your adolescent in that way. What would your adolescent say was different about you when you reacted to him/her that way?

_____

_____

_____

5. When you see your child this evening, promise yourself, "Whatever she says or does, I will react to her as if she were a very dear friend whom I want to keep for a very long time." Allow her to see you as that kind, caring friend who will always be there for her, no matter what. Think about doing this exercise with your partner as well, only for this evening. When it works, do it again and again.

Parenting Young Children: Externalize and Mesmerize

Externalizing problems with children helps them control their actions and helps you see the *problem* as the problem, not your *child* as the problem. In *Narrative Means to Therapeutic Ends*, Michael White and David Epston note that externalizing problems enables people to separate from the dominant stories that have been shaping their lives and relationships. They assert:

As persons become separated from their stories, they are able to experience a sense of personal agency; as they break from their performance of their stories, they experience a capacity to intervene in their own lives and relationships.

Viewing the problem as the problem helps me speak to children in the following manner about issues such as anger, grief and responsibility. The words in italics are the externalized problems:

"On Tuesday, the attitude that often gets in the way of you and Mom talking wasn't there. That's great. How were you able to be in control?"

"Tell me how you were so strong on Monday night that you didn't allow your fears to keep you from sleeping in your own bed."

"I am so impressed that you didn't let your anger bother you at home with your little brother."

"I think it's amazing that you didn't let your grandmother's passing keep you from your school work."

"Your energy certainly was under control as you did your chores today. How did you manage to stay on track?"

By talking about the problem in this way, you give your child an opportunity to conquer the problem through new actions. You can also help by collaborating on how you will conquer the problem. For example, if your child is afraid of sleeping in his own bed, you might consider saying:

"Joey, I know sometimes the fear of the dark bothers you and pushes you out of your bed and into my bed. Let's talk about what you and I can do just tonight so that the fears don't bother you as much and you become stronger than them."

First, notice how I spoke of the fear as something outside of Joey and blamed the fear for pushing Joey out of his bed. I then asked Joey to think of ways to become stronger than the fears just for one night. Going slowly helps children see progress. Perhaps Joey sleeps four hours in his own bed that night. The next day, instead of pointing out that he couldn't stay in his bed all night, it will be more helpful to say:

"Joey, I am so proud of you! You were stronger than the fears for four hours last night. How did you manage this?"

Each time Joey stays in his bed longer, it will be important to praise him. If he gets up sooner, instead of feeling as if things are going backward, tell him:

"That's okay. Fears are hard to fight. You fought them for two hours tonight. That's really great."

In the case of school issues, speaking to a child who has Attention Deficit Disorder (redescribed as "energy") and her teacher in this manner can be helpful as well:

"Ms. Taylor, I'm interested in hearing about the times when Susie's energy is more in control. Can you watch today for times in the classroom when she is concentrating slightly more and is not as distracted? I will ask Susie to watch for times when she is more in control as well."

By talking in this way, the teacher will know that you are viewing Susie differently. Perhaps when the teacher stands by her, she concentrates better. Maybe Susie completes certain assignments that are not as overwhelming. Susie may also have to be seated in a better area of the classroom to achieve a better outcome.

Twenty Years in the Future: Remember Me Well

In lieu of a divorce, Barbara brought her husband Dave to therapy. His job as a jeweler had recently become overly stressful. He expressed his frustration and stress by opening the kitchen cabinets and then slamming them shut, over and over again. Dave would then make other loud noises and yell at his wife and five-year-old daughter, Cecilia. Soon, Cecilia began having nightmares and trouble concentrating in school. Barbara told Dave that unless he changed his actions, she would leave him.

When I met Dave, I could tell he was less than thrilled to be talking to me. After my usual questions and conversation, I still wasn't sure I was making contact with him. I asked about his job and whether he had a tendency to blow up and become frustrated at work.

DAVE: No, I can't blow up like I do at home at work or I would lose my job.

LM: Are you saying you never get upset at the store?

DAVE: Hardly ever. I do get really stressed by certain situations, like when customers want me to redo things after they've told me what they wanted the first time.

LM: How do you deal with situations like that?

DAVE: There's an alley in the back of the store where I go on my break. I smoke a cigarette or chew tobacco and curse to myself until I calm down.

LM: I wonder … you seem like the kind of father who would value his little girl and wife at home as much as those customers and your boss.

DAVE: Sure, but home is where you vent. My father vented, and so did my mother. I ought to have a place where I can let it all out.

LM: I'm going to ask you both a question, but I don't want you to answer it. I just want you to think about it for the next week until I see you again. Let's go twenty years into the future. A reporter wants to interview Cecilia about what her life was like at age five, living with Daddy and Mommy. Over the next week I want you to think about what you hope she tells that reporter.

There was an eerie silence. Then they left.

The couple returned a week later. Barbara reported that Dave had been "as quiet as a mouse" and that Cecilia had had only one nightmare. I was delighted, and asked them what had happened to make the week so much better. Dave looked at me and said:

DAVE: You know that question you asked us? It hit me like a ton of bricks. I don't want my little girl thinking about me in any way but a good way.

As a parent, what you do every moment of the day, week, month and year is imprinted on your children. Imprint what you want them to remember about you. Do something with them today that you hope they'll remember fondly. In fact, do something every day.

Conclusion

There are as many different ways of parenting as there are children. If you can't recall when you parented effectively, *ask your kids*! They know. You won't lose face or seem incompetent. Quite the opposite. They'll respect the fact that you asked them. They may even suggest a harsher consequence than you gave them. Build that relationship. Be there when they need you. Go to their sports games and their band concerts. Talk to their teachers and know who their friends are. Become such a part of their life that someday when they too are adults, they'll remain connected to you.

My husband and I have three children, and at the time of writing, two are attending college and one is working while attending graduate school. Throughout their child and adolescent years, they each taught us that they needed to be parented differently. Our oldest, Roger Jr., responded better when we talked very seriously to him about his actions. Our daughter, Kelli, required time to herself to realize what she needed to do about an issue. Our youngest, Ryan, needed simple, defined actions and boundaries in order to make changes. It sometimes felt like a "hit or miss" game plan, but learning what worked has rewarded us well.

In his book, *The Seven Habits of Highly Effective People*, Steven Covey recalls a friend who learned how to handle his relationship with his son:

> I have a friend whose son developed an avid interest in baseball. My friend wasn't interested in baseball at all. But one summer, he took his son to see every major league team play one game. The trip took over six weeks and cost a great deal of money, but it became a powerful bonding experience in their relationship.

My friend was asked on his return, "Do you like baseball that much?"

"No," he replied, "but I like my son that much."

> The first and great commandment is, Don't Let Them Scare You.
> —*Elmer Davis*

Chapter Eight

Take Control Over Harmful Habits

The chains of habit are too weak to be felt until
they are too strong to be broken.
—*Samuel Johnson*

According to Webster, "a *disease* is a particular destructive process in an organism with a specific cause and characteristic symptoms". A *habit* is "an act repeated so often that it has become automatic with a person". Harmful habits interfere and sometimes destroy lives. Diseases are seen as pathological and can be treated only by experts. While substance abuse can be described as either disease or habit, it is helpful for a person in this situation to choose a description that opens up the possibility for change. This chapter will refer to substance abuse as a harmful habit, rather than a disease. Habits can be broken.

When in the grip of harmful habits like drug and alcohol abuse, eating disorders, excessive gambling or sexual misconduct, people usually seek traditional ways of getting help. They may experience confrontation, in-patient psychiatric treatment or day treatment. All of these methods direct the person to face up to her disease in the hope that realization and revelation about the negative effects will discourage her from continuing.

When people don't comply, they're said to be in denial or "not ready for change". Therapy often stops at that point and people are often told that there's nothing else to do until they're ready to change. This method of counseling has been very successful, primarily for people who want to stop using substances. Unfortunately, for just as many, it hasn't worked. In their book, *Working with the Problem Drinker,* Insoo Berg and Scott Miller describe working differently with substance abusers. Instead of looking at substance abuse as a disease, they focus on people's strengths and relationships as in the following example:

> Mr. Z maintained that he did not have a problem with alcohol, and further, that he did not want to stop drinking. When asked, he freely admitted having made many promises to stop drinking that he had subsequently failed to keep. According to Mr. Z, however, he really had never wanted to make such promises in the first place. He reported that most often after making such promises, he would visit his parents who owned a local tavern. While there, he would decide to have "just one drink". Then, feeling guilty for having broken his promise, he would stay at the tavern and drink even more … the therapist began to explore what was different about those times when Mr. Z did not drink … both Mr. and Mrs. Z agreed that there were times when drinking was not a problem and that such times had a beneficial impact on them individually and as a couple.

What Does Your Drug Do for You?

I worked with Marina, a twenty-three-year-old woman who used methamphetamines on a daily basis. She admitted it was jeopardizing her relationship with her current boyfriend, her job as a salesperson and her health but she continued the habit, despite her desire to quit. At our first meeting, she asked me:

MARINA: Why do I do this when I know it's harmful and destructive to my life? There must be some deep-seated reason that keeps me doing this over and over even though I know it's wrong.

I asked her what using the drug *did* for her.

MARINA: It gets me through stress. It helped me sell, sell and sell some more in my last job and that got me ahead in the company. It also helped me to make more money and feel confident about myself. I had so much energy when I used that I accomplished everything I wanted to at home.

Her reply was an answer to The Miracle Question, which was asked differently in this case. It was a simple answer, but she was unhappy with it because it meant that she needed to deal with her life. Our time together focused on ways to help her get through stress, accomplish tasks at home, learn how to maintain and succeed in a job and begin feeling confident about herself while being drug-free.

When dealing with harmful habits, The Miracle Question involves searching extensively for *exceptions,* times when the habit is not occurring. People are told they have the resources to stay habit free by identifying situations in which the habit does not take over. This gives them a chance to see their situation as temporary as they search for the times when these habits don't rule them. They do this by identifying the following about themselves:

- Personal abilities that help the person accomplish goals without turning to the harmful habit for assistance.

- Situations when the harmful habit does not take over and interfere with life, relationships or work.

- Instances when the person is able to refuse using the habit through helpful thoughts and situations.

Try Walking the Walk to Solutions

The following excerpt from my book *Solution Focused Group Therapy* describes how using the process of The Miracle Question can assist someone bothered by alcohol abuse. It helped a man identify what he needed to do to " walk the walk" to solutions:

> John, aged 33, came to group therapy at the insistence of his parents. He had moved back home after losing his eleventh job in three years. Financially strained, he depended on his parents for shelter and food. Through boredom, he'd sell some item of worth to buy alcohol and would binge at a friend's house for days at a time. Then he'd return home, where his parents lectured and nursed him back to health.

He described his life as nothing but torment. He told the group that he refused to go to AA (Alcoholics Anonymous) and to forget about giving him a lecture—it wouldn't work. He talked at length about how he wanted his life to be. I acknowledged his need to drink to numb the pain from difficulties he had experienced over the past five years. His wife had left him, he had repeatedly lost jobs, his property had been repossessed and his health was failing. John *knew* alcohol was the culprit. I attempted to help the group step into his world and also to let him know we were trying to understand. At the end of the session he said: "This is the first time I have met a counselor who did not scold me. I know I have a problem... I never needed anyone to tell me. Here I feel like you can really help me because I'm not embarrassed to tell you about all of the stuff I have done. It seems like you understand."

At least it seemed to be a beginning for John. Over the next few sessions, he talked of times when he had not been drinking and of the activities he'd enjoyed then. He had a black belt in karate, and during his non-drinking times, he would work out and feel good. He also described how he used alcohol to help him sleep. From his earliest memory, he was too hyperactive to sleep well. Alcohol relaxed him into a three-to-four hour sleep per night. I referred him to a sleep disturbance clinic where he began evaluation.

While he was processing other exceptions, he looked at me and said, "I binge when I'm hiding my booze. I was so afraid my wife or my mother would catch me, I would drink to hide it." This realization led him to conclude that perhaps being on his own again, supporting himself, might lead to a better chance of gaining his sobriety again. He began searching for a job, found one, and earned enough money after two months to move out of his parents' home. The drinking slowed to one or two drinks per weekend, according to our contract, and he began working out again at a karate studio.

John stopped coming to group when his life improved. Over a year later he called to tell me that he had relapsed. I coached him to think about his former strategies and complimented him on his initiative to call me and get back on track.

John joined a new chemical recovery group shortly after our phone conversation. It was fascinating to hear him describe how he kept his job over the past year. At first he focused on how he had failed. He had difficulty giving himself credit, yet the group complimented him on his commitment to keep his job and on his concern for his parents. Through group observations John eventually learned that he needed to socialize with the co-workers whom he had previously thought were out to get him and begin working out in a new karate studio. Whenever he revealed his fear of being close to a person at work, the group reassured him that they enjoyed his company and suggested he follow his own instincts. The group helped solidify his immature beliefs about his competency and helped him to believe in himself.

When John began to learn more about his ability to cut down on his alcohol use, he felt more confident and successful. Typically, people struggling with drugs and alcohol abuse are often searching for ways to stop pain in their lives or to find an alternative way of dealing with daily problems such as insecurity or loneliness. Eventually, an addiction happens where they physically need the substance. Instead of talking about the harmfulness of alcohol, which didn't affect John's drinking at all, I focused more on how his life would be when he gave up his harmful habit. That was much more attractive to him than admitting activities he had chosen were wrong. Doing that is a blow to anyone's self-esteem. It seems to work better to focus on how life will be—how others will react when the habit is under control.

Stop Denying The Denial

The following case shows another example of using this approach with a family member who has a problem with substance abuse. In this family, the daughter, Jane, had tried unsuccessfully to help her father, Barry, see that his drinking was harming everyone in the family. Often referred to as "the scapegoat" by some alcohol prevention programs, she had acted out, been defiant toward her family and developed other symptoms which led to everyone else seeing *her* as the problem. This often occurs as a young person attempts to raise the red flag over the family as a cry for help. In an effort to gain confidence from the family and lessen any resistance, I approached them with the intent of externalizing Barry's drinking. I use this approach when I want to learn more about how the family maintains the problem as a way to enlist everyone's cooperation in tackling the situation.

The family tried to convince Barry he was an alcoholic. He denied such allegations, saying he provided a good home, food and clothing for them. He didn't have a problem with alcohol—they had a problem in not appreciating him. With other families present, I asked Jane, mother Anne, and younger daughter Alexis:

LM: How do you wish things would be for your family in the near future?

JANE: Things would be normal … like everybody else's.

LM: What would it look like someday soon when it is normal?

JANE: I could depend on my father to take me to the place I asked him to take me the day before, without his forgetting. He would spend time with me instead of drinking at night. He wouldn't yell at my mother.

LM: When were things better in the past?

JANE: It was better when he had a different job.

LM: It sounds like a problem has invaded your household in the past few years. How has the problem changed things?

JANE: Like I said … he forgets things I tell him, he yells …

LM: What do other people do with this "problem"?

JANE: My mother cries and yells back. I get mad at Dad and scream at him. Then I go to my room and get depressed. My little sister acts up. I run away sometimes. I'm in trouble a lot.

LM: Suppose everyone began fighting the problem on a small scale. What would you each see yourselves doing?

ANNE: I guess I wouldn't listen to his yelling. I would leave the room when it starts instead of yelling back. I probably would stop buying the beer.

JANE: I would go out with my friends more and not stay around and be as depressed. If he stopped drinking I would probably behave better around him.

ALEXIS: I think I'll stay away from Daddy when he is drinking instead of asking him to play with me. He doesn't like to do it then. I would play by myself.

DAD: I guess I could try drinking less at night. I still don't think I have a problem but it sounds like everyone else does. I love them all and I really want them to be happy.

LM: Barry, it sounds like the problem has caused you to do things you don't like. How would you like things to be for your family? How do you want them to view you?

This change of focus from seeing Barry as the problem to interpreting the *problem* as the problem helped lessen resistance among family members and increased opportunities to try new approaches. Notice how the conversation was never confrontational toward Barry. Yet, as he listened to how "the problem" was affecting everyone, his suggestion was to slow down on the drinking. Ideally, of course, stopping the drinking would have been more advantageous to everyone. But giving up a habit that had ruled the family's life and given Barry relief would have been difficult.

The family continued counseling and Barry was asked to watch for signs that easing up on his drinking was making a difference at home and that he was beginning to be more appreciated. I told him to take note whenever he saw a change in behavior in the form of a direct "thank you" to him for his efforts. I asked him to keep a daily journal describing how everyone was reacting to his drinking less. After two weeks, he chose to drink only occasionally after seeing the dramatic changes in each family member's behavior. His wife stopped buying beer and with that money, she invited her husband to start socializing with friends who did not drink.

Jane lost her attitude, did as she was told at home and chose better friends. Alexis gained her playmate back. Barry told me that he had never felt as appreciated as he did now. His family told him the same.

The following ideas and questions can serve as a guide for using The Miracle Question to begin gaining control over harmful habits such as drug and alcohol abuse, eating disorders, excessive gambling or sexual misconduct or any other habit that is intruding in your life.

NOTE: If you or someone close to you is experiencing *severe* physical symptoms of use or withdrawal from substance abuse or severe weight loss or gain from eating disorders, please see a physician as you begin this plan. It is vital to have professional assistance as you begin altering your approach to dealing with the habit that is keeping you from enjoying and participating in your life.

Exercise 8.1: Ideas for Gaining Control Over Harmful Habits

1. Attempt to understand the need to use the substance.

What has the harmful habit done for you?

_____

_____

_____

_____

_____

How has the habit jeopardized your involvement in the following situations?

Family:

_____

_____

_____

_____

Job:

_____

_____

_____

_____

Health:

_____

_____

_____

_____

2.   Visualize your life without the harmful habit.

What will you do someday soon when the habit is no longer a concern for you and others in your life?

_____

_____

_____

_____

_____

Who will probably notice first that the habit is occurring less and that you are in control?

_____

_____

_____

3.   Explore past attempts to gain control over the habit.

What have you tried in the past to control the habit? These are the exceptions.

1. _____

_____

_____

2. _____

_____

_____

3. _____

_____

_____

4. _____

_____

_____

_____

5. _____

_____

_____

Place a check mark by the attempts that worked for a short time. Mark through the attempts that did not work.

Think how you were able to accomplish each of the items you checked. Think of who was there, where you were, or what was different in any way.

1. _____

_____

2. _____

_____

3. _____

_____

4. _____

_____

5. _____

_____

For the exceptions you listed above, write what you believed about yourself that might have made a difference:

_____

_____

_____

_____

4. Task Development

On a scale of 1 to 10, in which 1 means you are taken over by the effects of the harmful habit and 10 means you are in control of the habit, where were you before beginning this process today?

Habit is in control   I am in control of the habit

← →

    1   2   3   4   5   6   7   8   9   10

Where would you like to be tomorrow? _____ By next week? _____ How will you get there? Use the answers from question 3 to develop your new strategies against the harmful habit.

_____

_____

_____

_____

_____

_____

_____

_____

Place a check mark next to items that you can do for the rest of today. What thoughts and beliefs do you need to keep in mind as you finish today?

_____

_____

_____

_____

The Weight Loss Experts: Looking at Anorexia Differently

Eating disorders seriously affect people who are either denying themselves nourishment in order to be thinner or overeating to gain a feeling of satisfaction. Professionals agree that the majority is searching for control over their eating habits, particularly when other areas of their lives seem out of control. Using the process of The Miracle Question, people bothered by eating disorders are given the chance to see that the habit is in control of them, not vice versa. This approach often helps people whose fragile grip on life stems from the desperate need to be in control of their weight and thus, their life.

The following case describes Kim, a 5' 7" eighteen-year-old woman who weighed seventy-five pounds. Reading through the case, you'll notice I rarely use the diagnosis of *anorexia* nor do I refer to Kim as having an eating disorder, as the connotation of a *disorder* means the person needs to be repaired. I want the person to feel in control, able to repair herself. Rarely does the description of the diagnosis and its probable outcome give a person enough of a reason to stop a habit that *does something for her.* Rather, a description of a *habit that discourages health* is more helpful. Again, a habit can be broken. A disorder can dog the person and keep her from believing in her competencies. This excerpt is from my book, *Solution Focused Group Therapy:*

When I first met Kim, she was beginning to experience chills, amenorrhea and hair loss. Her physician had become alarmed when her parents brought her in for a physical after she returned from her college freshman year in Paris. Clothed in several heavy shirts during the heat of summer, she relayed her fear when, the night before, she had looked in her mirror and had seen her ribs. Frightened, yet not fearful enough to begin to eat heartily, she said she was very concerned about gaining weight, because she had once weighed over one hundred thirty pounds and did not want to reach that weight ever again. She reported that all of the foods in Paris contained fatty ingredients so her diet there had consisted solely of apples. She also described her parents as over-protective and financially stressed and she also had a brother who had strayed into drugs, disappointing his family tremendously. A bright college student who had made all A's during her first year abroad, Kim described the years prior to college as stressful and competitive, attending an elite preparatory school where she felt an outcast. As the conversation continued during our initial group assessment session, I learned the following about Kim and her goals:

- She wanted to raise her low self-esteem, which she felt she had developed from trying to be the perfect child after her brother so disappointed her parents.

- She was fearful of food and saw only fat grams whenever food was presented to her by her well-meaning parents … then she refused to eat.

- She wanted to be healthy again, but not fat.

- She wanted to get back into life, but wanted to control how she did so.

- She knew there was a problem with her eating habits, but she did not want to describe it as an eating disorder.

- Counting calories and pieces of food was helpful to her because it gave her a sense of control.

- Weight gain would have to be a gradual, controlled event that she was willing to do, slowly.

- She said she wanted permission from me to respect her need to be thin, yet healthy.

After several individual therapy sessions, Kim stabilized her weight loss and slowly began to eat fat-free, healthy meals that she chose to eat on a daily basis. While her parents desired a quick weight gain program, I spoke with them (with Kim's permission and insistence, and her doctor's approval) and cautioned them against pushing her into gaining weight too rapidly, thus respecting her need for control. Kim said she wanted to gain weight at her own pace, and I agreed that she had a good idea, reassuring her that she was indeed *'a weight loss expert'*. I mentioned casually that, in the future, should she regain her weight too quickly, she would certainly know how to lose it again. She had, after all, lost fifty pounds during one year and I told her that convinced me that she would know how to control any weight gain that got out of hand. She shyly agreed that she had this expertise and continued to count calories, occasionally asking me if that was acceptable. I always replied the same: 'How does it help you to eat more healthy foods?' She always replied: 'I feel more in control.' The times (her *exceptions*) when Kim ate were:

- *When she knew the exact caloric intake of each item.*

- *When she planned her meals for the next day, making sure that one meal was not as high in calories as the other two.*

- *When she ate alone, she felt relaxed and was more likely to eat.*

- *When she felt organized in her day.*

- *When her parents backed off about her eating and said nothing about the fat-free foods she ate.*

- *When she recalled how seeing her ribs had frightened her.*

Kim regained thirty pounds during our visits over nine months. She became vibrant and healthy, yet I continued to refer to her whenever I saw her as 'the expert on weight loss'. This continual reminder that she had control made an impact. She eventually entered a support group and began using the same phraseology with others who struggled with the same issue of control.

The following ideas will help you examine a harmful eating habit that may be jeopardizing your health.

NOTE: If you are experiencing dramatic weight loss, please contact your physician to gain reassurance that you are not jeopardizing your health. Seek professional counseling from someone you trust and who respects your personal goals.

Exercise 8.2: Ideas for Dealing With Harmful Eating Habits

1. Attempt to understand the need for the harmful eating habit. Ask yourself:

What has participating in the harmful eating habit done for you?

_____

_____

_____

_____

_____

_____

How has the habit jeopardized your involvement in the following situations?

Family:

_____

_____

_____

_____

Job:

_____

_____

_____

_____

Health:

_____

_____

_____

_____

2.   Visualize your life without the harmful eating habit.

What will you do someday soon when the habit is no longer interfering with your health and others in your life?

_____

_____

_____

_____

Who will probably notice first that the habit is occurring less and that you are in control?

_____

_____

_____

_____

_____

3. Explore past attempts to gain control over the habit.

What have you tried in the past to control the harmful eating habit? These are the exceptions.

1. _____

_____

2. _____

_____

3. _____

_____

4. _____

_____

5. _____

_____

Place a check mark by the attempts that worked for a short time. Mark through the attempts that did not work.

Think how you were able to accomplish each of the items you checked. Think of who was there, where you were, or what was different in any way.

1. _____

_____

2. _____

_____

3. _____

_____

4. _____

_____

5. _____

_____

For the exceptions listed above, write what you believed about yourself that might have made a difference:

_____

_____

_____

_____

_____

4. Task Development

On a scale of 1 to 10, where 1 means you are taken over by the harm-ful eating habit and 10 means you are in control of the habit, where were you before beginning this process today?

Habit is
in control

I am in control
of the habit

| 1 | 2 | 3 | 4 | 5 | 6 | 7 | 8 | 9 | 10 |

Where would you like to be by tomorrow? _____ By next week? _____ How will you get there? Use the answers from question 3 to develop your new strategies against the harmful eating habit.

_____

_____

_____

_____

_____

_____

Place a check mark next to items in the last question that you can do just for the rest of today. What thoughts and beliefs do you need to keep in mind as you finish today?

_____

_____

_____

_____

What can significant others do to assist you just for today?

_____

_____

_____

What is the best method of asking them to do this for you?

_____

_____

_____

_____

Conclusion

The idea of thinking differently about harmful habits does not minimize the severity of a problem nor discount the diagnosis of a "disorder". The ideas in this chapter simply offer fresh ideas and observations that may lessen the impact of the behaviors on a person's life, freeing that person to believe life can indeed change. The difference in thinking of a person as bothered by a dangerous habit instead of afflicted with a disease can help him talk about the situation more comfortably, lessen embarrassment and promote hope and possibility. Instead of thinking of yourself as crippled and controlled by a problem or diagnosis, you can begin to perceive your life as reparable and worthy of your participation and focus on it.

Believe that life is worth living, and your belief will help create the fact.
—*William James*

Chapter Nine

Rewrite Your Life After Trauma

*Experience is not what happens to you; it is what you do with
what happens to you.*
—*Aldous Huxley*

Several years ago, I worked with a group of sexual abuse survivors. Carrie, aged twenty-four, was married to Todd, who
sexually abused her on a regular basis. They were childhood
sweethearts and the abuse didn't occur until after their marriage.
Currently separated and fearful of more abuse, she struggled with
how she was going to have to say no to reconciling with him one
more time.

Carrie was a successful second year elementary school teacher,
who also worked part time at a store to distract herself from the situation and avoid Todd. This strategy was exhausting her. I commended her for her strength and showed her the timeline (to be
introduced later in this chapter), inviting her to think about how
life could be when she stepped out of the cycle of abuse, fear and
exhaustion. As our session ended, I asked her if anything we did
during our time had made a difference. She replied:

CARRIE: I never realized that it was even possible to permanently
   get away from this until now.

Two weeks later she returned to tell us Todd had confronted her
about a reconciliation, but she had turned him down and filed for
divorce. She had quit the part-time job and, for the first time without fear, was beginning to enjoy swimming in the pool at her apart-
ment complex. She had placed a restraining order on Todd, who
was finally leaving her alone. She had answered an advertisement
for a national airline, applied for a flight attendant position and

was hired on the spot. This group session would probably be her last as she was due to begin training in two weeks.

Stepping Out of the Story

I believe that people have the ability to heal and move forward after experiencing abuse. This belief has evolved from witnessing the success of many clients who did this in spite of their terrible experiences with abusive situations. Many were able to develop good relationships, get married, have children and become successful in their careers. It helped some survivors to confront their perpetrators and reproach them for the damage they had caused. Others said they preferred to move away from those who hurt them. It seemed more helpful for each person to choose an individual path that worked for him instead of being told what needed to happen.

While the memories never totally disappeared, their influence lessened over time and the determination to have a better life was unstoppable, guiding these people forward into lives they once thought were impossible to attain. They are some of the bravest, most amazing and competent people I will ever know. They are the true teachers of survival.

Perhaps you often wonder why it happened to you. Many of my clients do. Those conversations about *why* the abuse happened are often accompanied by shame and doubt, as if they were responsible in some way for the abuse. They ask:

"Why did it have to happen to me?"

I usually reply:

"I don't know. I do know that you *did nothing to cause the situation to happen to you. Tell me, if you did know why it was done to you, how that would help you to step back into life?"*

In his book, *Residential Treatment*, Michael Durrant asserts that therapy should be about identifying some recognizable problem and modifying people's behavior or dealing with the underlying causes. He believes therapy should be about establishing conditions in which people can think of themselves differently, and thus, respond differently.

Instead of searching for reasons why the abuse happened, it is more helpful to understand what the survivor will need to do, think or believe about himself so that he can move forward with his life. But before identifying those needs and mapping out a new story, it is important to view oneself *differently*. Changing the description of a person who has experienced abuse from *victim* to *survivor* can serve as a beginning. It can allow the person to see how her self-description directly impacts her beliefs about herself and thus, her actions. The following exercise is adapted from my book *Solution Focused Group Therapy* and has been modified for individual work in this book.

Exercise 9.1: Are You a Victim or a Survivor?

1. Imagine how you would like your life to be one month from now. You would still have the same people and circumstances in your life, but your actions would not be as influenced by the "situation". Write your new ideas below:

    _____

    _____

    _____

    _____

    _____

2. What we believe about ourselves in the present can affect our actions. As you think about your goals, imagine how you would be acting, believing or feeling if you thought about yourself as a victim while trying to reach the goal. How would you act, believe or feel as you pursued your goals, thinking of yourself as a survivor? Write your answers below under the corresponding label:

Victim	Survivor

Actions:

—

—

—

—

Beliefs:

—

—

—

—

Feelings:

—

—

—

—

3. Which description, victim or survivor, seemed to be most helpful as you thought about accomplishing your goal?

   I want to think of myself as a _____.

4. Where in your life have you successfully used these actions, reactions or beliefs in other situations? Consider times at home, work, with children, friends or family. How were you able to do this? What would others say you did? Please be specific.

_____

_____

_____

_____

_____

_____

_____

_____

_____

_____

5. On the timeline below, envisage the event that tried to take over your life. Mark an "x" on the line to represent when the event ended. Below your "x" write how the event has kept you stuck in your life.

    Write the typical age or lifespan of your family relatives at the end of the scale. Now, as you look forward, stepping out of the event that kept you stuck, count how many years you will have to escape from the event.

    Realize something now. You are smarter, wiser and you know more about life today than you did when the event occurred. You will never have to go back to that time when you were threatened because you want more in your life than to choose similar circumstances and relationships.

$$\longrightarrow$$

Birth   End of life

How the event has kept me stuck:

_____

_____

_____

_____

Now begin to think about your life in this new way, as a chance to do what you want to do and with whom. Write your heart's desire for yourself below:

_____

_____

_____

_____

6.   The Action Plan:

What would you and I see you doing, specifically, in a very small way, just for the next week or two that would tell us both that you were indeed stepping out of this situation?

_____

_____

_____

_____

_____

_____

Losing Someone and Finding Him Again

If someone dear to you has died, you know the feelings of loneliness and emptiness. It may seem that part of yourself has been lost as well as the person you loved. Perhaps you're trying to say goodbye to the one you lost. Maybe others are telling you to put the experience behind and move forward with your life. This is of course easier said than done. Freud says that in order to heal from loss, people have to incorporate the meaning, influence and experiences of the person lost *differently* in their lives. They must realize that the person left behind became who he is as a result of knowing the person who has died.

To see yourself as someone influenced by the lost person and as having an opportunity to carry on that person's influence and legacy is not only healing, it is a celebration of the person whose life has ended. The next exercise is dedicated to you and your loved one.

Exercise 9.2: Say Hello to the Memories and Let Them Help You Live Each Day

In his article, "Saying Hullo Again", Michael White suggests the importance of empowering oneself after a loss, using the influences of the lost person productively. White suggests the questions below for persons dealing with a new reality. The questions marked with an asterisk (*) are my additions so that you might answer them in the form of Action Plans. Their purpose is to help you to say hello to the person who is gone.

If you were seeing yourself through your loved one's eyes right now, what would you be noticing about yourself that you could appreciate?

* I would appreciate that I am:

_____

_____

_____

What difference would it make to how you feel if you were appreciating this in yourself right now?

* When I am appreciating this about myself, I will:

_____

_____

_____

_____

What do you know about yourself that you are awakened to when you bring alive the enjoyable things that your loved one knew about you?

* My loved one helped me to realize that I am:

_____

_____

_____

_____

What difference would it make to you if you kept this realization alive on a daily basis?

* If I remembered what my loved one saw in me each day I might:

_____

_____

_____

_____

_____

What difference would feeling this way make to the steps that you could take to get back into life?

* When I kept in mind what my loved one liked about me each day, I would:

_____

_____

_____

_____

How could you let others know you have reclaimed some of the discoveries about yourself that were clearly visible to your loved one and that you personally find attractive?

* Other people would realize that I have reclaimed my life when I:

_____

_____

_____

_____

Conclusion

If you have experienced trauma in your life, realize that you are a survivor, not a victim, ready to continue your life and write it differently. If you have lost someone you cared for deeply it's my hope that you continue the legacy and traditions that person gave you, starting today and throughout the rest of your life. Each day you participate in your life and remember a saying or belief that person gave to you, you keep that person alive in your heart and spread her value and influence to others. My best wishes to you as you engage in the journey of saying hello to someone who has said goodbye to you.

> Ancient Egyptians believed that upon death they would be asked two questions and their answers would determine whether they could continue their journey in the afterlife. The first question was, "Did you bring joy?" The second was, "Did you find joy?"
> —*Leo Buscaglia*

Chapter Ten

Your Miracle Journal

You cannot solve a problem with the same kind of thinking
that created it.
—*Einstein*

Each time you write in this chapter, add what you were thinking or believing when your exceptions occurred. As I mentioned earlier, mere thoughts can be the difference that makes the difference. Change your thoughts and you change your perceptions—and that makes the actions easier. These discoveries hold great meaning for you. They will become part of your solutions. On the following pages, write the exceptions you have experienced today when things worked better. It will become your Miracle Guide.

Exceptions:

_____

_____

_____

_____

_____

Thoughts, beliefs and actions that helped you to achieve the above exceptions:

_____

_____

_____

_____

_____

_____

If you planned to repeat what went well today, what would you do? Include what would you need to think or believe about yourself or others so that you were successful. What would other people say you'd need to do?

_____

_____

_____

_____

_____

_____

_____

_____

_____

_____

_____

_____

_____

_____

_____

_____

Bibliography

Berg, I. and Dolan, Y. (eds.), 2001, *Tales of Solutions: A Collection of Hope-Inspiring Stories*, W.W. Norton, New York.

Berg, I. and Miller, Scott, 1992, *Working With The Problem Drinker*, W.W. Norton & Company, New York.

Covey, S., 1989, *Seven Habits of Highly Effective People*, Simon & Schuster, New York.

de Shazer, S., 1985, *Keys to Solution in Brief Therapy*, W.W. Norton & Company, New York.

Glasser, W., 2003, *Warning: Psychiatry Can Be Hazardous to Your Mental Health*, HarperCollins, New York.

Haley, J., 1976, *Problem Solving Therapy*, Harper & Row, New York.

Johnson, S., 1998, *Who Moved My Cheese?*, Putnam Publishers, New York.

Metcalf, L., 1997, *Parenting Toward Solutions*, Prentice-Hall, New York.

Metcalf, L., 1999, *Solution Focused Group Therapy*, The Free Press, New York.

Minuchin, S. and Fishman, C., 1981, *Family Therapy Techniques*, Harvard University Press, Cambridge, MA.

O'Hanlon, W. and Weiner-Davis, M., 1989, *In Search of Solutions*, W.W. Norton & Company, New York.

Quindlen, A., 2000, *A Short Guide to a Happy Life*, Random House, New York.

Stanley, T., 2000, *The Millionaire Mind*, Andrews McMeel Publishing, Kansas City, Missouri.

White, M., 1989, *Selected Papers*, Dulwich Centre Publications, Adelaide, South Australia.

USA, Canada & Mexico orders to:
Crown House Publishing Company LLC
4 Berkeley Street, 1st Floor, Norwalk, CT 06850, USA
Tel: +1 203 852 9504, Fax: +1 203 852 9619
E-mail: info@CHPUS.com
www.CHPUS.com

UK, Europe & Rest of World orders to:
The Anglo American Book Company Ltd.
Crown Buildings, Bancyfelin, Carmarthen, Wales SA33 5ND
Tel: +44 (0)1267 211880/211886, Fax: +44 (0)1267 211882
E-mail: books@anglo-american.co.uk
www.anglo-american.co.uk

Australasia orders to:
Footprint Books Pty Ltd.
Unit 4/92A Mona Vale Road, Mona Vale NSW 2103, Australia
Tel: +61 (0) 2 9997 3973, Fax: +61 (0) 2 9997 3185
E-mail: info@footprint.com.au
www.footprint.com.au

Singapore orders to:
Publishers Marketing Services Pte Ltd.
10-C Jalan Ampas #07-01
Ho Seng Lee Flatted Warehouse, Singapore 329513
Tel: +65 6256 5166, Fax: +65 6253 0008
E-mail: info@pms.com.sg
www.pms.com.sg

Malaysia orders to:
Publishers Marketing Services Pte Ltd
Unit 509, Block E, Phileo Damansara 1, Jalan 16/11
46350 Petaling Jaya, Selangor, Malaysia
Tel : +03 7955 3588, Fax : +03 7955 3017
E-mail: pmsmal@streamyx.com
www.pms.com.sg

South Africa orders to:
Everybody's Books CC
PO Box 201321, Durban North, 4016, RSA
Tel: +27 (0) 31 569 2229, Fax: +27 (0) 31 569 2234
E-mail: warren@ebbooks.co.za